GOD
GOT HIS HANDS
DIRTY

A Prelude to Revival

BOB BROCK

GOD
GOT HIS HANDS
DIRTY

A Prelude to Revival

BOB BROCK

Empowered Publications Inc
Millry, Alabama

Published by:
Filled Books
An Imprint of Empowered Publications Inc.
529 County Road 31
Millry, Alabama 36558

Library of Congress Control Number: 2017

ISBN: 978-1-943033-53-9 (paperback)
Digital edition ISBN: 978-1-943033-54-6 (eBook)

Dedicated to my family without whom
this book would not have been possible.
To wife Yvonne,
my son Reggie, my daughter-in-law Connee,
my daughter Cindy, and my son-in-law Darius.
Thank you for your support
through many years of ministry.
May you experience your own personal revival.

Contents

ADDENDUMS

Foreword

Revival...What is it? Why should we pursue it? Where will it occur? When will it happen?

How can it be experienced? Who can usher it in? These are just a few of the questions that have been posed to me, in one form or another, over the last 17 years of evangelistic ministry. In our current church culture, revival has been misunderstood, misrepresented, misused, and because of such is now missing in action.

As well, the ministries of the evangelist and prophet have been perverted, problematic, and powerless thus destroying the biblical potential for these God ordained offices. "And he gave some, apostles; and some prophets; and some, evangelists; and some, pastors and teachers..." (Ephesians 4:11 KJV) Some no longer believe that the aforementioned are applicable or relevant in today's culture. Others have never been biblically educated in, nor experienced, the benefits produced by these scriptural precepts, persons, and practices. Yet, there are many who desire to reap the natural/spiritual bounty produced through revival, evangelists, and prophets, but they are hindered by a lack of information and handicapped in implementation.

Thus, I have partnered with my friend Bob Brock in the production and publication of this book. Brock has served in ministry for some 60 years. He has functioned in multiple roles, including that of pastor and evangelist. His ministry experience has spanned the gamut of large church/small church, rural/urban, seeking revival/experiencing revival/pastoring revival. You will gain an appreciation for Brock's gifts as both a writer and communicator, via the instruction and inspiration to be discovered in the content of this discourse.

The reader will realize that *revival* is not limited to a prescribed number of services specified on the church calendar. Nor, is it delivered by the act of any particular charismatic personality.

Rather, revival will be defined through the lens of biblical characters, circumstances, and concepts. Then, you will be equipped with the tools to properly and prayerfully assess the condition of your church in relation to revival. Finally, you will find BOTH spiritual and practical application which will combine the truth, time, talent, and treasure of the pastor, congregation, and evangelist/prophet producing a potent New Testament result.

It is our desire that this book serves the local church, the grassroots pastor, and the itinerant minister in fulfilling our God given purpose one to another, as well as our communities in need of Christ. Together, we are better!

"Will you not revive us again, that your people may rejoice in you?" (Psalm 85: 6 MEV)

-Evangelist Jason Stidham-

A Personal Note From The Author...

I launched my ministerial journey in an inauspicious fashion. Soon after leaving a college campus, I was invited to preach a two weeks' revival for a very brave man that wanted to give me an opportunity to spread my wings and soar, or at any rate, to spread my wings. I didn't have an automobile. So I carried a rather weather worn suitcase and a Bible, and boarded a Greyhound bus. I didn't have a computer or attaché case bulging with powerful well used sermons. It was just me peering with wide eyes out the window of a bus, a suitcase, and a Bible.

In those days, revivals were at least two weeks in length and often longer with no Saturdays off. I didn't have a dozen dress shirts and a fresh suit to wear in each of the services. I had wash and wear clothing before wash and wear clothing was given that name. I came with what I had, not knowing what I needed, but I had something in my heart that was burning to tell people about Jesus. Each sermon was a fresh sermon and not a re-run. It was all I had and turned out to be all I needed. The Lord did the rest.

I discovered that if I would do the best I could with what I had, God would do the rest—and He did. Gradually revivals have gone from two weeks, to one week, then to three days, and in many cases now 1 day only, or perhaps just one service on Sunday morning. This trend has not evolved because the world is getting better, but because the church is no longer expecting the best from revival. To avoid embarrassment from negative impact, the church stopped scheduling revivals.

My colleague and friend, Dr. Gene Burgess, tells the story about a parade which had one float's sponsor form that was simply signed, "SPONSORED BY THE HOLY SPIRIT." This is the driving force behind this book. We are praying that the fires of revival will begin to break out across America and the world again with this indisputable signature: Sponsored by the Holy Spirit.

Our Heavenly Father wants to show off for His church. He wants to be the SPONSORER OF REVIVAL to sweep over your city, and to break barriers which hold back His power big enough to break every chain of sin, mighty enough to perform miracles, powerful enough to push back the darkness of doom and gloom, vigorous enough to deliver from vice, stout enough to heal sicknesses and diseases, tough enough to stifle the diabolical schemes of terrorists, and robust enough to bring revival when it seems impossible.

Come Holy Spirit and bring revival.

-Bob Brock-

The First Church of the Almost Dead

<u>Timeline</u>: 120 days before the start date of scheduled revival

<u>Perspective on revival</u>:

Most pastors/churches/denominations are much like the woman who went into her doctor's office to get the report of her recent X-rays. The report wasn't good. She needed surgery but couldn't afford it. So the doctor touched up her X-rays. This made her feel better temporarily, but it was disastrous in the long run. I am afraid that is true of most pastors/churches/denominations when taking an honest look at the condition of our church. We would rather have the X-rays of our diagnosis touched up if the diagnosis is not good. It may make us all feel better, but it is tragic for days, years or generations to come. It's pay now or later.

<u>Proposal</u>: Be honest with the diagnosis of the church, accept the findings and fix the problems. The answer is: revival now!

"The First Church of the Almost Dead" is not a flattering name. Few people, if any, would be attracted to it. Unfortunately, it can be applied to many churches today. They haven't put a padlock on the doors and they are still going through the motions, but they are lifeless, listless, and languishing away. Everyone knows they are almost dead. Everyone but them.

In American society, there are 9 churches closing every week. Church leaders are faced with the pressure of turning a church around with limited resources to reach new people, hire effective leaders, and pay all the bills. Pastors are frustrated because the doors are closing before they can achieve the vision God gave them.

An article in the New York Week described it like this. "When the saints go marching out."

The Religion Editor of CNN recently wrote, "The Millennials are leaving the church in droves."

In the 1980s, Ross Perot spoke about the national budget deficit as "the crazy aunt living in the basement that nobody wanted to talk about." We have our own "crazy aunt" — tens of thousands of dead or dying churches. Like that "crazy aunt," we love her. We want to treat her with dignity. But, ultimately, we think she is hopeless and best ignored. John characterized this sad situation by writing the following words in Revelation 3:1-2. "And unto the angel of the church in Sardis write: these things saith he that has the seven Spirits of God, and the seven stars; I know your works that you have a name that you are alive and not dead. Be watchful, and strengthen the things which remain that are READY TO DIE." Not dead but dying!

> *God has an answer for the church that was on the ropes and sucking down oxygen just to keep the doors open.*

That's what God said, not a church consultant specialist, but God has an answer for the church that was on the ropes and sucking down oxygen just to keep the doors open. It's all in Heaven's diagnostic report.

Number 1, be watchful. (3:2) It is just another way of saying, "Be aware of what's happening to you. Be honest about what you see. Don't ignore the obvious." If you listen to ministers greeting each other at a conference, you would think everything is GREAT. How are you doing? Great. How is the church? Great. They are not intentionally exaggerating or stretching the truth. They must be speaking by faith and living by the rule of II Corinthians 4:18 which says, "While we look not at the things which are seen, but at the things which are not seen; for the thing which are seen are temporal; " If you look at the ecclesiastical scene in general, things are not so great. God has given us eyes to see, and I trust that we will be honest enough and wise enough to acknowledge that many churches are in a critical crisis.

Number 2, remember. (3:3) Remember the promises of God which will not fail. Remember the person and work of the Lord Jesus Christ. John encouraged us to remember our first love and reclaim it. Jesus taught us the Holy Spirit would bring things to our remembrance. The words of Haggai should haunt us to a certain degree. He asked the people of his generation, "Who saw the house in its first glory? How do you see it now?" Then he answered his own question like this. It is nothing by way of comparison. (Haggai 2:3, 9)

The Psalmist had a fond recollection when he wrote, "I call to remembrance my song in the night..." (Psalms 77:6) He also said, "I have remembered thy name in the night..." (Psalms 119:55) It was when Peter "remembered the words of Jesus" that it brought tears of repentance to his eyes. No doubt these are precious times that Peter had in mind when he wrote these words to believers who needed to be revived. "I stir up your minds by way of remembrance." (II Peter 3:1)

Kevin Arnold explained memories beautifully when he said, "Memory is a way of holding onto the things you love, the things you are, and the things you never want to lose." The First Church of the Almost Dead needs to have a resurrection of memories and hold on to the ones you don't want to lose.

Number 3, repent. (3:3) It means a change of mind and heart which includes a change of direction. It means that we will make things happen rather than to hope things will change for the good. It means I will not continue to do certain things and will make every effort to do some that I may not have done before. Henry Ford said, "If you always do what you've done, you'll always get what you've always got."

When true repentance takes place, it turns loose of trusting our feelings and stands fast on faith which is the daring of the soul to go farther than it can see.

Repentance means I will use God power instead of man power.

When true repentance takes place, it turns loose of trusting our feelings and stands fast on faith which is the daring of the soul to go farther than it can see.

Number 4, strengthen the things that remain. (3:2) This is a command to do something for those who are almost dead. It means to revive and become spiritually alive again. The Bible declares that the church at Smyrna was dead (past tense) and is alive (present tense). (Revelation 2:8) Thank God there is hope for the terminally ill churches who are on Spiritual Hospice care. Strengthen it. Revive it. Send the "shock treatment" of the quickening power of the Holy Spirit through it, and it will live again.

Ezekiel heard this command direct from God. "Son of man can these bones live? And I answered, O Lord God you know. So I prophesied as I was commanded: and as I prophesied, there was a noise, and behold a shaking, and the bones came together, bone to his bone. Then said he unto me, prophesy unto the wind, prophesy, son of man, and say to the wind, Thus saith the Lord God; Come from the four winds, O breath, and breathe upon these slain, and they may live. So I prophesied as he commanded me, and the breath came into them, and they lived, and stood up upon their feet an exceeding army." (Ezekiel 37:3, 7-10)

The musty old mausoleum, The First Church of the Almost Dead, became a recruiting station for a mighty army for God. The mortified was glorified; the anesthetized was mobilized; the paralyzed became a power ball.

There's a difference in evangelism and revival. Evangelism is an all-out effort to reach the lost, and revival is an act by God to revive believers. Evangelism can mean knocking on doors to tell people about Jesus, but revival is opening the doors for the King of Glory to come in. (Psalms 24:6-10) It is God with us witnessing by his power, wooing by his love, waiting to bless, warning of sin and winning over the enemy.

What is a revival? Interestingly enough, I was shocked when different people reminded me that this generation doesn't even know what revival is. It's like asking what's a mimeograph machine or a Sputnik? Most people don't seem to know or perhaps even care.

Since this has happened more than once, I have been mortified and mystified as was Jeremiah when he wrote these soul chilling words. "Is it nothing to you, all you that pass by?" (Lamentation 1:12) Passivity for revival has replaced passion. Vices drove out victories. Misdirection and malfunction of leadership have baffled the benevolence of Heaven. The leaders on earth refused to confine themselves to the instructions of Jehovah, altered their message, and eliminated their uncompromising jealousy for the King and His kingdom. The purposes of heaven have been prostituted. Don't blame the people. They don't make the rules, fill the schedules, and pick the speakers.

The Watchman went blind. The shepherd gathered his likeminded buddies around a committee table and as dictators *plot a short way to truth and a broad way to heaven* while the sheep were being devoured by wolves. The priest that was responsible for keeping the fire on the altar burning carelessly let the fire go out. What an inexcusable tragedy. The very fires on the altar that moved kings to give up their thrones, warriors to surrender their swords, and drug lords to close up shop were smothered out by craving for modern methods, conveniences, and artistry. These things become a substitute for the fire of revival and swap glory for glitz. It cheapens grace, muzzles the Holy Spirit, and smothers free spirited worship.

The question is WHY do people not know what revival is? That really bothers me. Did they know what tithe is when they first started attending church? Or how many books there are in the Bible? Is Job an employment opportunity? Is the rapture a Science Fiction movie? What is the Sacrament? Is being born again a trick question? Is 666 a domestic or foreign oil company? How did they find out what these things mean?

> *Is Job an employment opportunity? Is the rapture a Science Fiction movie? Is 666 a domestic or foreign oil company?*

The answer is very simple. They were taught. We usually look at Romans 10:13-15 as a technique for missionary presentations of the Gospel to people on the other side of the hemisphere. "How shall they call on him in whom they have not believed? And how shall they believe in him of whom they have not heard? And how shall they hear without a preacher?" How do people learn about tithing, etc.? Someone explained it. Someone gave priority to making sure they know how the plan works so the church can pay its bills.

Why do people in this generation not know what revival is? I read this in Pew Research. "*The older generation of Americans are not passing along the Christian faith.*" No one has told them. They have not seen genuine revival modeled. Revivals faded away automatically just as would tithing and water baptism if teaching on these subjects ceased or gradually became less and less a part of our mode of operation and curriculum. When we went mum on the subject of revival and scheduling revivals and gave revival a different name, they were quietly buried without a decent funeral. The Word says, "How shall they believe" if they <u>have not heard</u>.

> *When we went mum on the subject of revival and scheduling revivals and even gave revival a different name, revivals were quietly buried without a decent funeral.*

I am crying out with the same passion that AP Collins had in 1915. He said, "The demand for a revival is imperative; the need is urgent; danger is imminent…there is a trumpet call to the Church—to angel or messenger of the Church—to repent and do the first work, because he has left his first love. Nothing is more in divine order or according to the divine purpose than a revival."

With Moses of old, I am asking God to, "show *ME* thy glory." (Exodus 33:18) Jesus declared, "Blessed are the pure in heart; for they shall see God." (Matthew 5:8) That's what I call glory which is *a visible manifestation of an invisible God.* One man declared, "True revival is that divine moment when God burst upon the scene and displays his glory…the glory comes when God takes over. He fills the church with His presence and power." It is more than a

> *Glory is the visible manifestation of the invisible God.*

funny feeling or fabrication of a deranged mind. It's God in action doing things that only God can do. The beloved writer of Psalms 19:1 recoded the following powerful words concerning the "glory of God." "The heavens declare the glory of God; and the firmament sheweth his handiwork."

God is unseen but revealed by what he scrolled across the expanseless skies above our heads. Every time you look up, the heavens are shouting from God saying, "I'm here, and my creation is evidence." God speaks to us in the glory of His healing. He whispers to us in miracles. He discloses himself to us in lives that are eternally changed by his grace. He communicated to us by demonstrating His love upon the Cross.

The Bible says, "The heavens DECLARE the glory of God." According to Merriam-Webster's Collegiate Dictionary, the word DECLARE means "to make visible or clear; to make known formally, officially or state emphatically." God did not take his glory and stuff it into a dark, damp, bat cave in South America or bury it deep in the Indian Ocean. Rather, He created a gigantic decoupage and stretched it 25,000 miles to completely circle the globe. He wanted the heavens to declare the glory of God so that if one were shivering in the icebox of the Antarctica, scaling the forbidden mountains of Tibet, scorching in the burning hot sun of Death Valley, or snoozing under a Palm tree in Hawaii, ALL THEY WOULD NEED TO DO IS LOOK UP and God would be saying, "I am here, and I am the Creator behind creation."

He wanted the glory to be in the White House and flop house, in the class room and court room, in the barn yard and jail yard, in the crime lab and science lab. The glory is not only the presence that emanates from Christ but the things he does that leaves his fingerprints all over it. I don't see the baker, but I enjoy the bread he bakes. I don't see the cobbler, but I wear the shoes he makes. I don't see the Creator, but I see His signature written all over creation. It's His glory shouting to us day and night.

The glory of revival is the hope for the First Church of the Almost Dead. It's the Resurrected Savior who faced and tasted the dread of death and survived, and is alive ever more. What we need is not a pretty, dignified funeral for the First Church of the Almost Dead, but a new beginning from the womb of revival. I am praying for you and your church with the beautiful words penned by Amy Carmichael: "Make me Thy Fuel." "Give me the love that leads the way, the faith that nothing can dismay, the hope no disappointments tire, the passion that will burn like fire, let me not sink to be a clod: Make me thy fuel, Flame of God." Amen.

> *What we need is not a pretty, dignified funeral for the First Church of the Almost Dead, but a new beginning from the womb of revival.*

Action Steps To Revive The Church Of The Almost Dead.

First, we must <u>IDENTIFY</u> the causes for the slow death of the Almost Dead Church. This list would no doubt include but not be limited to:

- Indifference
- Impiety
- Ignorance
- Introversion
- Irrelevance
- Insomnia

Secondly, <u>INTERCEDE</u> for the church whose light is failing and survival is in doubt.

Intercede for *illumination of God's word* in their hearts and head.

Intercede for *intensification of worship and praise.*

Intercede for *personal intimacy with God.*

Intercede for *inspiration to replace boredom.*

Intercede that the *inharmonious spirit* will be broken.

Finally, <u>IGNITE</u> a fresh passion for God.

Ignite a passion for loving *God with renewed fervor.*

Ignite a fire of *thanksgiving to God for his goodness.*

Ignite the fire of *evangelism to reach the lost.*

And ignite a *spark of revival that will break into a flame that no one and nothing can extinguish.*

"Act as if it were impossible to fail."
-Dorothea Brande-

*"It shall be done for them of my
Father which is in heaven."
-Jesus – Matthew 18:19)*

Who Can Tell What God Would Do If...

Timeline: 90 days before the revival start date

Perspective: No borders or boundaries nor ceilings or floors can limit what faith in God can do.

Proposal: Do all you know to do and see what God can do. Any limitations are ours. God has none. Trust Him and see.

Albert Einstein touched a very private compartment of my heart when he said, "Imagination is your preview of life's coming attractions." It's the vision of my soul touching the untouchable, reaching the unreachable, and thinking the unthinkable. It's seeing God without limits, hope without boundaries, and freedom without fetters. It's me wondering out loud and writing it down on this paper. I wonder what God would do if...

> *It's seeing God without limits, hope without boundaries, and freedom in the Spirit without fetters.*

If we count our blessings and not our crosses; if we learn to listen and listen to learn; if we get up one more time than we fall; if we don't care who gets the credit; if we gave God our all and not just the left overs; if we earnestly endeavored to forgive and forget; if our thanksgiving exceeded our want list to God; and if we worship God with abandon. I know, it's radical. But who can tell what God would do if we would all give it a try?

God uses radical believers to tackle radical challenges utilizing radical efforts to get radical results. It's a common characteristic of what genuine revival looks like. Paul referred to such leaps of faith

23

as foolish in the eyes of a fault finding, disapproving crowd. Noah was a numbskull for building a huge ship and had nowhere to put it in or get it near to water deep enough to float it, but God brought the water to him. Daniel was considered to be a nincompoop when praying was against the rules, but he had a divine visitation when he was thrown into a flaming inferno and didn't get a blister on his body. Angels were arrowheads to predict that Sodom was going to be turned into an ash heap in a matter of hours. Jesus was a buffoon to talk to a dead man and tell him to get up and walk out of his grave. It sounded crazy until the dead man crawled out of his burial pajamas and came strolling out of the midnight darkness of death.

> *It sounded crazy until the dead man crawled out of his burial pajamas and came strolling out of the midnight darkness of death.*

Paul addressed the radical who dared to wonder what God would do if we turned all the results to Him when he wrote, "I came to you, came not with excellency of speech or of wisdom…and my speech and my preaching was not with enticing words of man's wisdom, but in demonstration of the Spirit and of power; that your faith should not stand in the wisdom of men, but in the power of God." (I Corinthians 2:1,4,5)

Radical Christians are not satisfied with pomp, pageantry, and entertainment without the power of God being demonstrated. They simply express and believe that:

> *Radical Christians are not satisfied with pomp, pageantry, and entrainment without the power of God being demonstrated.*

Every good and perfect gift comes down from God out of heaven. (James 1:17)

It is God that gives power to get wealth. (Deuteronomy 8:18)

God will not withhold any good thing from them that walk uprightly. (Psalms 84:11)

Nothing is impossible with God. (Luke 1:37)

God has the will and authority to fulfill all of his promises. (Romans 4:21)

The effectual fervent prayer of a righteous man avails much. (James 5:16)

Being radical means casting off the yoke of bondage in worship, conciliating broken relationships, contending for the faith once delivered to the saints, calling those things which are not as though they are, conquering complacency, and celebrating the glorious, victorious name of the Son of God.

I love reading the story of the fearless foursome in Mark 2 that models characteristics of people who will stop at nothing to see signs and wonders.

Characteristic Number 1: They had radical ASPIRATIONS to witness the miraculous. Mark 2:3 paints this picture in living colors.

> *They aspired to interrupt the usual, break through the normal, and tap into the supernatural.*

"And they come unto him, bringing one sick of the palsy which was borne of four." By modern standards, this religious gathering was a resounding success. The most talented, popular speaker of that era was filling the pulpit. A standing-room-only-crowd packed the lecture hall. Everybody who was any body was hanging out there, but 4 people had aspirations beyond breaking attendance records. They aspired to interrupt the usual, break through the normal, and tap into the supernatural.

They were possessed with the spirit of Elijah who stood on the banks of a flooding, forbidding river looking to the other side where the Promised Land was and with unflinching faith declared, "Hereby you shall know that the living God is among you." (Joshua 3:10) That's what revival is—knowing that the living God is among us.

Characteristic Number 2: They were consumed with radical ASSUMPTIONS – <u>God has no limits.</u> Mark 2:9 records the words of the Wonder Worker himself who said, "Whether is it easier to say...thy sins be forgiven thee: or to say, Arise, and take up thybed and walk?" It makes no difference with God. He can do either with ease. We must then assume that what HG Rolls declared it true. "His throne of majestic power is invincible. His priesthood is indestructible. His promises are immutable. His salvation is incorruptible. His covenant is irrevocable. His spiritual blessings are innumerable, and His help knows no bounds." Radical always gives the advantage to God, regardless.

Characteristic Number 3: They were radically AGGREESSIVE —nothing could stop them. Examine Mark 2:4 carefully. "They uncovered the roof where he (Jesus) was: and they let down the bed wherein the sick of the palsy lay." They refused to let anything stand in their way. Aggressiveness for revival must not wane or waver when we are going against the tide. Jesus said, "And from the days of John the Baptist until now the kingdom of heaven suffereth violence, and the violent take it by force." (Matthew 11:12)

I am inspired to quote the aggressive challenge that Winston Churchill made to his countrymen during a dark, dark moment in World War II. In sheer radical determination, he said, "We shall not flag or fail. We shall go on to the end. We shall fight in France, we shall fight on the seas and oceans, we shall fight with growing confidence and growing strength in the air, we shall defend our island, whatever the cost may be. We shall fight on the beaches, we shall fight on the landing grounds, we shall fight in the fields and in the streets, we shall fight in the hills; we shall never surrender...Let us, therefore, brace ourselves to our duties, and so bear ourselves that if the British Empire and its Commonwealth last for a thousand years, men will still say, This was their fines hour."

Oh, men and women of God, may this be our finest hour in asserting our God given right to contend for an old fashioned, up to the minute, God sent revival.

Characteristic Number 4: We must not forget that they experienced radical AFFIRMATIONS OF FAITH – that is to say, positive, miraculous results. "Arise, and take up thy bed, and go thy way..." (Mark 2:11) We must remember that the world will never be changed by the mere sound of words. It will only be changed by the Wonder Worker and He is still on the job. Jesus stamped these words in the Good Book, and they can never be erased. "These signs shall follow them that believe:" (Mark 16:17) It is a promise. This is a believer's right and privilege. We are believers.

Yes, we are each only one (so was Jonah), but we can be one that counts and makes a difference just as one shingle in a roof counts—as one link in a chain counts—one brick in a wall counts. I pray with you that God will hear us as we pray as someone once prayed, "I am only a drop make me a fountain; I am only a hill make me a mountain; I am only a serf make me a king; I am only a sprinkle make me a fountain; I am only a spark make me a fire." Amen.

Adoniram Judson dared to say what many of us may have wanted to say on many occasions. *"Let me beg you not to be content with the commonplace religion that is now prevalent."*

Nothing about the ministry of Jonah was common. He obviously didn't have a stately church in downtown Nineveh with beautiful stained glass windows. He was a street preacher. When I remember Jonah, I don't think first about a big church or a big fish. I think about a man who impacted an entire city with a word from God. A city found a Savior. May that be our legacy as well.

His original, personal plan had to be scrapped, and it takes a big man to admit it and alter his own plan, but his ego was crushed on his way down to hitting bottom. His security was jerked out from under him. He

> *When Jonah had nothing to depend upon but God, he discovered that God was truly his sufficiency.*

lost everything as they threw him over the side of the ship into the lashing winds and waves of a violent storm. I mean everything. He didn't have a tooth brush or change of clothes to his name. God didn't send a second fish to be a valet for Jonah. He had nothing to depend upon now but God, and he discovered that God is truly our sufficiency. God is our source. God is enough. He learned through a painful experience that "as thy days; so shall thy strength be. The eternal God is thy refuge, and underneath are the everlasting arms:" (Deuteronomy 33:25, 27) He learned more in a severe crisis in his ministry than he could possibly imagine.

He learned: God's <u>timing</u> is perfect. Had the fish gone one degree off course or been 5 minutes later to arrive on the scene, Jonah would have been buried in a watery grave and soon forgotten. His epitaph would be chiseled into the history book as a prophet who went AWOL from the army of God. But God's timing was perfect. The big fish was at the right place, at the right time, to rescue a man running from God.

I learned this lesson when God opened a door for me at the bottom of an escalator in an airport in St. Louis, Missouri. I was walking down the hall headed for the parking lot, but God had another plan. He turned my attention to a man of a different color and culture standing at the bottom of an escalator holding a small piece of paper between his fingers and a strange look on his face. It was at that moment, I heard that still, small voice whispering, "Speak to him." Speak to him? What would I say? Somehow, I came up with a very novel plan. "Good morning. How are you today?" Don't grin. I didn't need a college degree to initiate that brilliant plan or even have the 4 Spiritual Laws memorized.

The man graciously returned the greeting followed by a question. "Would you help me, kind sir? I am from central Africa traveling to Washington D.C. and don't know where to go from here." With that, he handed me this small note which was his directions to his next flight. I was relieved and replied that I would take him to his gate of departure. Then he asked me what I do. I told him I was a pastor. "What church," he asked. I told him the name of my church, and a great big smile swelled upon his lips. His eyes began to twinkle. "I am superintendent of that denomination in Africa, and God loved me so much that he brings a brother from my denomination to meet me at the airport and take me where I need to go." God's timing could not have been better. I pray this is your time and you are in the right place for a mighty move of God. Your steps and timing are directed by God.

God's <u>method </u>was customized for the need of the hour. A fish was the answer. A camel would have been useless. A donkey would have failed in its mission. A fishing boat would have been chewed up and spit out by the storm. God's method for preparing for the move of God in Nineveh was a stroke of genius. He prepared a great fish and the fish got the job done. The wind and waves had no adverse effect on the fish. God still has fish and men that obey His voice and methods to bring your city to its knees. GOD HAS NOT RUN OUT OF METHODS.

- He used a baby's tears to soften the heart of Pharaoh's daughter.
- He used a hand displaced from the rest of the body writing on the wall to sober a room full of drunks.
- He used an earthquake to bring a jailer to his knees.
- He used a puzzling dream to cause a king to call for the man of God.
- He used an unwed, pregnant virgin to bring the Savior into the world to whom eventually every knee shall bow and every tongue confess that Jesus Christ is Lord.
- He used hornets as air born warriors to blitzkrieg Pharaoh and grab his attention.

God has ample methods to bring revival but is looking for a man or woman to whom He can reveal His plan and demonstrate His power. I pray that you will be that person. Robert Breason stated it so beautifully when he said, "Make visible what, without you, might perhaps never have been seen."

> *God is looking for a man or woman to whom He can reveal his plan and demonstrate His power.*

His results are phenomenal. Jonah 3:5 says it all. "*So the people of Nineveh believed God…*" This is a preacher's dream and the devil's worst nightmare. Jonah wasn't a polished preacher but a powerful one. He had one message containing eight words. It had no illustrations but was easy to understand, and the people and the king BELIEVED GOD. Then the despot king threw out this challenging question:

> *This is the preacher's dream and the devil's worst nightmare.*

WHO CAN TELL WHAT GOD WILL DO if...(You fill in the blanks).

- Looking for loopholes to avoid revival becomes looking and longing for thresholds for revivals.
- Church was a place where you could find God and find it difficult to ignore or forget God.
- Sin was confessed and forgiven by God.
- Factions in the church were united in fellowship and faith.
- Marriages that were melting would be mended.
- The love of power would be overthrown by the power of love.
- The clock was turned off and freedom in the Spirit was turned on.
- Announcements were decreased and anointing was increased.
- Sensational productions were pushed off the stage to give way to substance and authenticity.
- There was a voracious appetite for the Word of God.
- Humility replaced gaudiness and haughtiness in pulpit and pew.
- The call to holiness was louder than the demand for happiness. Happiness won't get you to heaven but holiness will, and true holiness will bring you happiness.

Jesus is the centerpiece of our worship, the master piece of our theology, and the most powerful piece of our preaching. Who can tell what God will do?

I firmly believe that God will release the Lion Tamer to tame the demons of lustful passion, the Bright and Morning Star to beam the light of hope into the night of midnight darkness of despair, the Mighty God to flex His muscles and set the captives of sin free, the Only Wise God to help us find answers to the most perplexing questions life has to offer, the Balm of Gilead to heal the broken hearted, and the Rose of Sharon to bring beauty into your world of chaos and miserable mess.

> *I firmly believe the Lion Tamer will tame the demons of lustful passion, and the Mighty God will flex His muscles and set captives free.*

Yes. Yes! Who can tell what God will do?

There is no greater joy in Heaven nor should there be in the Church than the sheer, uncontrollable joy of seeing

- A toothless tramp being transformed by grace.
- Prostitutes purged from sin and purified through the precious Blood of Jesus Christ.
- Wretched winos waddling to an altar to find deliverance from sin and addictive behavior.
- Despised predators plead for and find Divine pardon.
- Creepy crooks confessing transgressions and being converted.
- Repulsive racketeers are redeemed.
- Sinners are saved.
- The lost are found and returned.

Jesus summed it all up in these beautiful words. *"In this rejoice not, that the spirits are subject unto you; but rather rejoice, because your names are written in heaven."* (Luke 10:20)

Strike up the band. Grab a tambourine. Put on your dancing

shoes. Shout for joy. Clap your hand for a new name has been written down in Heaven! Church, this is the time for rejoicing.

Action Plan:

1. Review the article on You May Not Need a Revival if... (ADDENDUM I) Now you must answer the question, Do we need a revival? Identify five things from this document that leads you to conclude that your church needs a revival.

2. If you conclude you need a revival, study the Work Sheet for Planning a Revival (ADDENDUM II), and begin to fill in the blanks. Proceed with the plan.

3. What is an Evangelist (ADDENDUM III) is an overview of what an evangelist is and some Biblical trademarks. What stands out most about who an evangelist is and what they do? How can this guide you in selecting an evangelist for a revival?

4. Pastor and evangelist relationship (ADDENDUM IV) is vital to a revival success. After having studied this paper, what value do you place upon Matthew 18:19 and how can you apply it to your desire for revival? The entire verse is pregnant with meaning, but please note the incredible results. If TWO agree it shall be DONE FOR them BY THE FATHER IN HEAVEN. You can't do it, but God can!

Prayer:

Dear God, we acknowledge that we need revival and that a true revival must come from you. It is not manipulation of emotions and marketing ingenuity. It is a Divine visitation and heavenly manifestations. It is surrendering our will and ways to you and releasing you from the box of normalcy and allowing you to break through the boredom of routine. It is our dependency upon you and forsaking our sins. It is more than announcing that an evangelist is coming to town. It is celebrating the majesty of God, expecting miracles, hearing and heeding God's Word, hoisting praise and thanksgiving to ring in the heavenlies, and making Jesus Lord and Savior of our lives. Let revival begin now in my heart and spread in, and thru, and out of our church in the precious name of Jesus I pray. Amen.

ADDENDUMS: (Refer to addendum in back of book)

I. You may not need a revival if...

II. Worksheet for planning a revival...

III. What is an evangelist?

IV. Pastor/Evangelist relationship

*"God's time for revival is the very darkest hour
When everything seems hopeless. It is always the
Lord's way to go to the very worst case to
Manifest his glory."*
-Andrew Gih-

"God Is Calling…"

<u>Timeline</u>: 90 days before the start date of revival

<u>Perspective</u>: As a minister, you are called, expected to be courageous, and ultimately to conquer. Your purpose must ever be to rise above the average, seek more than the normal, and accept daring challenges to overcome by the authority invested in you by the One who has called.

<u>Proposal</u>: Your calling makes you a sleeping giant. My challenge to you is: don't be a midget minister, a pygmy preacher, dwarf dynamo, or a stunted spiritual giant. Be all that you can be in God.

Our calling is important. I was unaware of the emphasis I placed on our calling until this chapter was finished. I then discovered that the words call, calling, and called appear 44 times in this brief chapter. I speak special blessing over "the called."

You are called to be different and make a difference. You may be a common man or woman in the eyes of the world, but you serve an uncommon God. A. W. Tozer challenges you to "Refuse to be average. Let your heart soar as high as it will."

Jonah 1:1 begins with this statement. "Now the word of the LORD came unto Jonah…" Any other qualifications and certifications pale in light of his calling. He was not called by a committee or hierarchy. Politics in the name of religion had nothing to do with it. Has God called you to preach? Has God called you to be His mouth piece down here in this jungle of misplaced values, melancholy, mischief minded, and mocking society? Has He invited you to handle the Word of God carefully and not deceitfully? Has He knocked on your heart's door to let Him in to work through you manifesting the works of God? Has He designated you to carry the banner of the Cross into enemy territory?

The Bible refers to your calling as being heavenly and holy. *This makes you an ambassador of the Almighty, a personal representative of the Redeemer, a diplomat of divinity, and an envoy of the Eternal God. There is no greater honor or trust.* Peter admonishes "give diligence to make your calling and election sure: for if ye do these things, ye shall never fall:" (II Peter 1:10) Paul wrote these words in I Thessalonians 5:24. " Faithful is he that calleth you, who also will do it." It is described like this in The Message. "The One who called you is completely dependable. If he said it, he'll do it."

Your calling makes you a sleeping giant that He is trying to wake up to accomplish what He has called you to do. Your calling should make you totally reliant upon God, defiant to any obstacles that stand in your way, and live in compliance with His will for your life. Watkinson surveyed the horizons of possibilities that we have to accomplish for God and wrote, "Large areas of our inheritance are unsown, un-reaped; all kinds of beginnings abide sorrowfully incomplete. We live in the strange world of the undone." God has called you to <u>do</u> the undone, <u>unwrap</u> the unseen, <u>untie</u> bondages, and <u>unseat</u> the devil's authority in your home and church. And you are not called you to be timid but bold; not weak but strong; not to fail but to succeed: and not to be a follower but a leader.

> *Your calling makes you a sleeping giant.*

As a Leader, I am regularly inspired by Paul's words in I Corinthians 1:26-28 (The Message). Look at them carefully and apply them to your personal calling. "Take a good look, friends, at who you were when you got called into this life. I

> *God has called you to do the undone, unwrap the unseen, untie bondages and unseat the devil's authority in your home and church.*

don't see many of "the brightest and the best" among you, not many influential, not many from high-society families. Isn't it obvious that God deliberately chose men and women that the culture overlooks and exploits and abuses, chose these "nobodies" to expose the hollow pretensions of the "somebodies"? That makes it quite clear that none of you can get by with blowing your own horn before God. Everything that we have—right thinking and right living, a clean slate and a fresh start—comes from God by way of Jesus Christ."

Thank God for my calling. How many times would I have quit had it not been for a divine call I have upon my life? Has that ever happened to you? Say every Monday morning? Then I recall what God said about my calling. "For the gifts and calling of God are without repentance." (Romans 11:29) That means that I may doubt my calling, but God doesn't. His gifts and calling are under full warranty. He will never rescind or cancel it.

The Bible makes it clear that we are called according to his

> *God's purpose for you is to rise above the average, seek more than the normal and accept daring challenges that only he can help you to accomplish.*

purpose (Romans 8:28) not mine. His purpose is to rise above the average, seek more than the normal and accept daring challenges. We must make an irrevocable decision to peruse that calling whatever it cost leaving all regrets behind. It was blind faith for you and Abraham. The Bible says, "By faith Abraham, when he was called to go out into a place which he should after receive for an inheritance, obeyed: and he went out, not knowing whither he went." (Hebrews 11:8) I must admit that I chuckled when I read this. Read the last 6 words again: Not knowing where he was going. (Paraphrase) I don't know how it was with you, but I sure didn't know where I was going. And I might add if I had known, I might have gone stone deaf to the call.

God didn't include a GPS or a detailed agenda with my call. It was much like the little girl I saw yesterday. Her mom pulled into a parking place, got out, unharnessed the little miss from her car seat, and gently sat her feet on the ground. The little girl didn't know where she was, or for that matter, didn't have any idea where she was going or how to get there. She was totally oblivious to the traffic danger, but lifted her little hand and waited for mom to clutch it and lead the way. She showed no signs of confusion nor paranoia. As long as mom held her hand and walked by her side, she was perfectly content without a worry.

You see, she wasn't qualified to get where she was going, but the person who held her hand was. Wow. That reminds me so much of the call of God. He doesn't always call the most qualified, but He holds our hand and qualifies the called. I stumbled across this yesterday, but it had no name attached to it so I can't give them credit, but it was just what I needed. "Jacob was a cheater, Peter had a temper, David had an affair, Noah got drunk, Jonah ran from God, Paul was a murderer, Gideon was insecure, Miriam was a gossip, Martha was a worrier, Thomas was a doubter, Sara was impatient, Elijah was moody, Moses stuttered, Abraham was old, and Lazarus was dead. God doesn't call the qualified, He qualifies the CALLED!"

> *God doesn't necessarily call the qualified, but he always qualifies the called.*

We are the called and must not dare be "complacently dissatisfied" to assume that the idea of revival is not a bad idea but cannot be achieved. Some of the most common rational for reaching this conclusion is that times have changed, taste demands something different, and temperaments set the stage for middle of the road compromise. The old stuff gives way to the new stuff. Revivals are caught in the middle and usually fade away.

We have been called to put our hands on the plow and not look back, to light a candle rather than curse the darkness, to resist the devil instead of relenting, to be the head and not the tail, and to be a winner and not a loser. This must ever be the CREED OF THE CALLED. "And we know that all things work together for good to them that love God, to them who are the CALLED according to his

> *The creed of the called.*

purpose." (Romans 8:28) Don't be felled by fear, stymied by style, silenced by the majority, or crippled by criticism. You are a conqueror. God said it. I believe it, and that settles it.

What happens next is on your watch, and who knows but what you were called for such a time as this? You are called to preach curses and plagues as well as blessings and prosperity, to preach holiness as well as happiness and hell as well as heaven. Your message will not always be a feel good, seeker friendly content, but don't ever forget that heaven in mercy has called you to be His mouth piece on earth. All heaven is standing on tip toes cheering you own to victory. Don't keep them waiting. Give them something to shout about.

God called Jonah to go to Nineveh (Jonah 1:2), but he went toward Tarshish and in so doing was moving away from the presence of Jehovah leaving him no promises to stand on and assuming the task on his own. This was not a misunderstanding on the part of Jonah. It was a calculated defiance to God's will and purpose for his calling. I can't say I blame him for turning his sights toward Tarshish instead of Nineveh. Demographically, it was probably a good choice. All church growth studies would have pointed in that direction overlooking the call of God. Nineveh was a preacher's graveyard and a city poised to soon be buried in the cemetery of history. It was not a back woodsy, country bumpkin, Neanderthal wide place in the road. It was the capital city of the kingdom of Assyria. This is what we know about it.

1. Jonah referred to it 4 times as a "great city."

2. It was recognized as a wicked city (1:2) known as the city of robbers, disregards for justice, depraved thugs and lawlessness.

3. Violence ripped the city to shreds and chilled the population with fear. (3:8)

4. It was also known as being corrupted by evil. (3:8, 10) I understand that it was founded by Nimrod which means let us rebel, and since that is true, they were fulfilling that prophecy.

Nineveh was not ready for an evangelist or expecting revival and neither was Jonah. Jonah had to have a *personal revival* before he would be prepared to be lead a Divine visitation to save an entire city from doom. This is a pattern that permeates Scripture. Revival starts in the Church, the pastor, and/or the evangelist not the other way around. God called Jonah to Nineveh. Where is the place where you have been called? Ignore everything else and go there.

Elijah was called to Cherith. This seemed to be a place of demotion rather than promotion. He had been in the limelight of all the action, but now being tucked away into no man's land. If this had been a church searching for a pastor and accepting applications, the mail box would have been empty. Cherith was the place where the temperature often exceeded 120 degrees by midday. The water was polluted and covered by scum. It wasn't beautiful and comfortable, but it was where God called him. It was not *Mount Rushmore* where pictures of presidents are carved artfully into rock and tourist are drawn there by the scores. *Sinai* would have been an interesting place where earthquakes thunder and where lightning zig-zagged across the sky holding all who saw it in awe but had he gone there he would have missed the miracle of God's provisions.

> God called him to Cherith and if he went anywhere else his provisions would have gone to a different address, and he wouldn't have been there.

This seems to be the standard procedure for special moves of God. The priests were to step into the flooding waters of Jordan first before the waters curled back forming a tunnel for the people to walk through on dry ground. The priests led the march around the walls of Jericho before they imploded. Remember it was Peter, the key note speaker in Jerusalem on the day of Pentecost, that stooped down to gaze into the empty tomb that our Lord had vacated, that stood tall to share the good news of a resurrected Savior to a flustered multitude.

Men and women of God must be lionhearted before they can lift the weak hearted, tender hearted, to mend the broken hearted, big hearted to melt the hard hearted and warm hearted to thaw the cold hearted.

The man (or woman) of God must personally know the God of man—Mighty God, Maker, Mender of broken hearts, Merciful and Miracle Worker. We must know Him as a soldier knows his weapon before he goes on the battlefield, as a surgeon knows his scalpel before he enters the operating room, and as a navigator knows his maps before he sails on the wide sea. Our need goes beyond knowing ABOUT Him. We can know about Him by tearing out pages from a history book, but Paul's passion was to KNOW HIM. (Philippians 3:10)

> *Men and women of God must be lionhearted before they can lift the weak hearted, tenderhearted to mend the brokenhearted, big hearted to melt the hard hearted, and warm hearted to thaw the cold hearted.*

Yes. He's the Son of God, the Son of man, the Just One, the Head of the Church, the Lord of lords, the King of kings, the Door to the treasure house of God's vast provisions, and the Key that unlocks the limitless power of God. He's all of this and more, but we also need to know that he is the "*egguos*" of all the promises of God. (Hebrews 7:22) That Greek word means that He is personally the surety, guarantee that God will never break His word and that every promise will be filled for certain. *That's what the bloody cross and empty tomb of our Lord insures.*

As a result, God's church is to be glorious and victorious. Jesus is *the energizer* to the weak and weary, the *harmonizer* of discord, *authorizer* of divine intervention, *sanctifier* for our sins and *sympathize*r for the hurting. He called us and will sustain us. No darkness of our culture can put out the glowing light of its influence.

> *Regardless of how desolate the future may look—the promises of God hold true.*

John R. Rice, the famous evangelist of yester years said, "*Present-day wickedness, apostasy, and modern civilization cannot prevent revival.*" Regardless of how desolate the future may look—the promise of God holds true.

If MY PEOPLE which are called by name pray...THEN will things begin to happen for the glory of God. Tramps will be transformed. Prostitutes will be purified. Sots will be sobered. The glory of God at work will fill cities and countries. Heaven will kiss earth, and the schemes of hell will be foiled. I *am not nearly so interested in the "end" time message as I am the "THEN" time,* and we pray that this will be our "THEN" time.

It doesn't matter how thick the darkness may be. Darkness can't blot out light. Light wins every time. God never intended for HIS CHURCH to be beaten up and limping into spiritual warfare as the clock of time runs out. My skin almost gets chill bumps when I listen to the words of Earle Sande after he had ridden the magnificent Man-O-War. He declared racing on the back of Man-O-War was like being on a runaway locomotive. The Church is to be gallant in battle and like a runaway freight train unstoppable by trivialities, unperturbed by the attitudes, unmoved by the things we can't control and unbending in controlling what we can. The song writer put it in Biblical perspective when he wrote, *"Like a mighty army, moves the Church of God."* Jesus declared, "I will build my church: and the gates of hell shall not prevail against it." (Matthew 16:18)

When this is obviously not the case, something is wrong and needs to be fixed. Rachael Evans of the Washington post made this astute observation concerning something which might be wrong with the church. She said, *"If churches want to get millennials in the pews, they should stop trying to make church "cool."* Then she continued, *"Churches struggle to bring in and keep worshippers, they often miss the point by making services a bigger show or offering give aways."*

I was so impacted by a blog I read from Pastor Andy Harris, and I quote the following. "I guess I just took for granted that true Christians should know the difference between a church and a night club, a church and a country club, a church and a rock concert, a church and a funeral home, a church and a theater, a church and a TV studio, a church and a museum, a church and a book of the month club, etc. The sad thing is most of the "world" DOES know the difference, but the "church" people are enjoying the ride! The question is, "Where are they headed?!"

- We need something fixed when preaching is palsied, praying is anemic, and worship and praise are comatose.
- Something needs to be fixed when we spend more time in a service making announcements than proclaiming the glorious Gospel.
- Something needs to be fixed when we are mesmerized by charisma and ignore character.
- Something needs to be fixed when we are inebriated with the aspiration of popularity than to be inebriated with the Spirit.
- Something needs to be fixed when control is more important than contrition, when compromise over rides convictions, and when conservatism is condemned and liberalism is lauded.

I agree with R. T. Ketcham who said, "Attend church but do not attend a church which prefers science to Scripture, reason for revelation, theory for truth, progress for power, reformation for regeneration, good for God, jubilation for justification, feelings for faith, paralysis for peace and politics for precepts."

Action Steps: Admit That You Are Called By God, Courageous In God And Conquer Through God.

This is the opportunity for the "called" to step up to the plate, accept their priesthood honors, and

(1) Recognize the drastic need for revival: (a) God's intervention is imperative and (b) removal of any and all hindrances.

(2) Resort to prayer for revival: (a) Unwavering faith to believe God to demonstrate His power and reveal His glory and (b) Pray for signs and wonders to open the eyes of unbelievers.

(3) Repent of personal sins which hinder revival: (a) repent of neutrality in seeking the favor of God and (b) overthrow of Satan's dominion.

(4) Rejoice in the hope of revival: (a) rejoice in the goodness of God (b) rejoice in the greatness of God and (c) rejoice in the grace of God.

"That cause is strong which has not a multitude, but one strong man behind it."
-James Russell Lowell-

When God allows a burden to be put upon you,
He will put His arms underneath you to help you carry it.
-anon-

We Need a Break Through

<u>Timeline:</u> 30 to 60 days before revival start date

<u>Perspective:</u> Perceived or real barriers must be broken down to experience the full favors of God in revival.

<u>Proposal:</u> Make a firm commitment to seek God with all your heart for a true revival. James Womack's words challenged me beyond words. He said, "Commitment unlocks the doors of imagination, allows vision, and gives us the "right stuff" to turn our dreams into reality."

Many times ministers and other church leaders feel like they are beating their head against the wall. Frustrations over whelm us. The battle seems to be going against us, not for us. Our best efforts appear to be falling flat on their face. The fact is: we need the *GOD OF BREAK THROUGH* to come through for us.

An article in Pew Research assessed the situation in the church and families as being "wobbly and badly bent."

Kenneth A. Briggs declared, "(The Bible) has become a museum exhibit, hallowed as a treasure but enigmatic and untouched."

More than 1,500 pastors leave the ministry each month.

Pastor Pete Wilson a dynamic, highly successful pastor of Cross Point Church in Nashville, Tennessee recently resigned. In his resignation, he admitted, "Leaders who lead on empty don't lead well...for some time I've been leading on empty...I'm tired, and I am broken..."

It took a big man with a big heart to make this confession, and I urge you to remember him and many others who walk in such worn out shoes.

Here are some specific reasons why we need a break through.

- Conventional wisdom is not producing needed results.

- What is good for the goose may not be good for the gander. One size doesn't fit all.

- Just getting by is not good enough.

- Working harder and longer hours does not seem to be the answer.

- Attending one more supercalifragilisticexpialidocious church growth conference makes you want to regurgitate.

- Paralyzed by systemic failure in function and ineffectiveness of the church at large.

- Blinded by normalcy bias.

We must have a break through before we see more ministers break down and more churches fall apart.

> *We must have a break through before we see more ministers break down and more churches fall apart.*

Let me fast forward to Isaiah 43 (The Message) and put it in your inbox. God, the Breaker, said, *"I've called your name. You're mine. When you're in over your head, I'll be there with you. When you're in rough waters, you will not go down. When you're between a rock and a hard place, it won't be a dead end...Yes, I am God. I've always been God and I always will be God. No one can take anything from me. I make; who can unmake it?"*

Study these therapeutic words carefully.

Does this describe where you are? If so, please read God's promises to you which will not fail. Read them orally, out loud to yourself. I have, and they put some wind under my sails again.

- When you are in rough waters....*you will not go down.*
- When you are in over your head...*God will be there.*
- When you are between a rock and a hard place...*it won't be a dead end!*

Now meditate on the words of Paul in I Corinthians 10:13. *"God is faithful, who will not suffer you to be tempted above that ye are able; but will with the temptation ALSO MAKE A WAY TO ESCAPE..."* It sounds screwy to the world, but remember the same crowd expected Peter to sink, Daniel to be eaten by a lion, Esther to be executed when she insisted on seeing the king, and Lazarus to be frozen by rigor mortis in the cemetery even after Jesus called him from the dead. They were all wrong. 100% wrong, but God was right and always will be.

On a comical note let me share a little story about the preacher who was so carried away with God's goodness that in his excitement misquoted Psalms 18:29. He said that the Psalmist declared, "For by thee I have leaped over troops and ran through a wall." After the service, someone questioned him about how he thought he could run through a wall. Without hesitation, he answered, *"It is up to me to jump and up to God to open a hole in the wall."*

It is time to leap and let God to make a hole in the wall of:

- ✓ Religiosity strangulation—having a form of godliness but denying the power thereof (II Timothy 3:5)
- ✓ The spirit of the anti-Christ infiltration-emphasis on ANTI-christ (I John 4:3)
- ✓ Advancement and acceptance of the doctrines of devils (I Timothy 4:1)
- ✓ Assaults against the Word of God – there is a growing tendency to attempt to discover a right way to do wrong things and to make things seem to be right that God says are wrong. (II Corinthians 4:1-2)
- ✓ Fading fervency and fascination with Jesus. (Revelation 2:4) Most of our church related problems will dry up and blow away if every Christian would fall in love with Jesus again.

✓ War between traditional and contemporary styles and manner of worship. This is not a pimple on the nose. It is a cancer devouring unity in the church.

Such is the condition that

> *This is more than a pimple on the nose. It is a cancer devouring unity.*

Jesus described as "a house divided will not stand." (Matthew 12:25) But considering this reality and realizing who (Jesus) said it has not produced an olive branch. There is no deed of amnesty; no comprehensible and conciliatory arrangements or reversal of conditions.

What we have on our hands and heart is a "super religious stalemate:" a wreck going somewhere to happen. We are reconciled with God, but fail to be reconciled with each other. Paul recorded these words in II Corinthians 5:18-19. "All this comes from God who settled the relationship between us and him and then called us to settle our relationships with each other...God uses us to persuade men and women to drop their differences and enter into God's work of making things right between them..." (The Message) Powerful words but seldom heard – God has CALLED us to settle our relationship with each other.

When I read this, it becomes evident there are two sides to reconciliation. *Horizontal* (reconciled with God) and *lateral* (reconciled with each other). Forgiveness is getting our hearts right with God.

> *Forgiveness is getting our hearts right with God. Reconciliation is getting our hearts right with people.*

Reconciliation is getting our hearts right with people.

It's amazing to try to comprehend what Jesus had to say about the importance of lateral reconciliation in Matthew 5:23-24. "Therefore if you bring thy gift to the altar and there rememberest that thy brother hath ought against thee: leave there thy gift before the altar, and go thy way; FIRST BE RECONCILED to thy brother, and then come and offer thy gift." God said, "Don't try to talk to me until you can talk to your brother." *Prayer ineffectiveness ends where reconciliation begins.*

A happy and healthy church is composed of a bunch of reconcilers who are not determined to have their own way but God's way. This is the break through that God and all heaven is waiting to give us. Our prayer will ever

> *Prayer ineffectiveness ends where reconciliation begins.*

be, "Not my will but thy will be done on earth as it is in heaven."

When we demand our own way in total disregard for God's will, we are vulnerable to two spirits standing in our way to revival and must be dealt with radically. They are a *lying spirit* (II Chronicles 18:21) and *the spirit of fear* (II Timothy 1:7). The lying spirit deceives us to believe something is true which isn't, and the spirit of fear prevents us from stepping out of our comfort zone.

Beware of the Lying Spirit

These are *SAINT SINS* that we sweep under the rug or look the other way. *The lying spirit* rips the heart out of any aspirations and anticipation that we can have revival: questions if God's word is

> *Imagine what the world would look like if Eve had told the serpent, "That's a lie."*

true, persuades us that we are wasting our time in serving the Lord and expect things are going to get better, scorns the idea that good will prevail, laughs at any insinuation that Jesus Christ is the same yesterday, today and forever, and mocks the insane notion that all things work together for good to them that love the Lord and are called according to his purpose.

Can you, in your wildest imagination, think about what the world would have been like if Eve had told the serpent, "That's a lie." But she didn't, and from that moment the world began to spin out of control. Had she challenged and renounced it, sin's pages within history would be blank, no tearstains would darken it's pages, no graves would've been dug, no hospitals would be built to battle diseases, no tornados would trigger the warning horns at the midnight hour, divorce courts would be empty, no debt of sin would be hanging over our head. There would be no hell to fear, and no need for Christ to suffer and die on the cruel cross. No sin. No sorrow. No death. No dread. No terror. No tears. No graves. No grief.

The devil is a liar and the father of all lies. He lied to Adam in the garden and continues to spread his lies today. His lies must not cause you to doubt that: you are the righteousness of God; you are more than a conquer through Jesus Christ; the God of peace shall bruise Satan under your feet shortly; and God will open the door of opportunity that no man can shut and that ALL THINGS are possible with God.

Don't believe the devil's lies. Your situation is not hopeless. Your city is not incorrigible, and your church is not impervious to a mighty move of God. Any other assumption is a lie from the pits of hell. Jesus declared, *"Ye shall know the truth, and the truth shall make you free."* (John 8:32) The truth will release you to overlook past failures, overcome fears, overflow with faith, overhaul your own attitude, and overtake the promises of God.

> *The truth will release you to overlook past failures, overcome fears, overflow with faith, overhaul your own attitude, and overtake the promises of God.*

Avoid The Spirit Of Fear

The spirit of fear works hand in hand with the spirit of lying. Once you believe the Devil's lies you are *unprotected from the spirit of fear.* You fear the future. You fear failure. You fear what's going to happen to your family. You fear becoming a financial flop. You fear friction that may arise in the church. You fear futility of efforts that will not be effective. You fear the fate of your ministry.

The Bible says, *"Fear hath torment."* (I John 4:18) Somehow I believe this communiqué is touching the heart of some pastor or church leader who is experiencing this fear torment right now. It shows up in the form of:

- Disappointments which are the abolition of joy.

- Discouragement that is an abscess of a victorious spirit.

- Defeat which is success turned upside down by the fury of tarnished trust.

- Despair which is being overwhelmed with hopelessness.

We must have a revival NOW to give you a break through. A break through will fortify you against frailty, fight back assaults on your freedom, and cause you to forget past failure. I speak II Corinthians 2:14 over you in Jesus name. *"Now thanks be unto God, which always causethh us to triumph in Christ..." Note the word ALWAYS. It's a promise you must claim:*

When we really believe that there are no hopeless situations and there are only people who have grown hopeless, we seize the moment of opportunity.

- Acknowledge the Sovereignty of God regardless of our circumstance.

- Believe in the sufficiency of God to meet our every need.

- Confess that victory is ours now in Jesus name.

- Glorify God when you really don't feel like it.

Joshua probably had the jitters walking in circles for 7 days around the imposing, defying walls of Jericho, but he kept walking.

Don't go by your feelings or necessarily by what you see. Joshua didn't see anything happening for 7 days and probably felt nothing but blisters on his feet, but he walked by faith not by sight. He walked as

Six days of failure didn't weaken his resolve.

seeing the invisible, feeling the intangible, and accomplished the incredible. *6 days of failure did not weaken his resolve.* All the snide remarks did not faze him, and all his critics did not dissuade him. He had his breakthrough. The walls came tumbling down.

I understand the importance of Paul's words in Galatians 6:9. "Let us not be weary in well doing: for in due season we shall reap, if we faint not."

I am fascinated to hear the voice of a distraught, weeping angel in Revelation 5:5. This perplexed angel faced a challenge that appeared to be insolvable much like the perplexity that some of us are facing.

The angel cried, *"Who is worthy to open the book, and to loose the seals thereof? And no man in heaven, nor in earth, neither under the earth, was able to open the book, neither to look thereon. <u>And I wept much</u>...."*

This is probably an oversimplification, but I will allude to this book as the book of the future.

The future was murky and unclear to them. They lacked a sense of direction. They couldn't open the book nor could they find a guru to do it for them. All they could do was weep. And you might note that this was a strong angel. This was not an angel afflicted with a personality weakness or psychological malfunction. They tried to open the book but all in vain.

Have you been weeping over your situation? Have you tried hard but failed? Are you frustrated, tired and faint? You may be encouraged to know that angels wept over frustrations, unanswered questions, and fruitless efforts.

> *Have you been weeping over your situation? Have you tried hard but failed?*

The same things that we weep over, right?

Then an answer came. *"Weep not; behold the Lion of the tribe of Judah, the Root of David, hath PREVAILED to open the book,"* What a relief. Weep not over your weakness, stop sobbing over your suspense, and crying over confusion.

This was not a pep talk or dose of psychological mind altering medication. There was a legitimate reason to alter their mood and dispel their melancholy. THE LION HAS PREVAILED, and He has power and authority to open the book. The Lion will PREVAIL today and give us a break through in:

- The plateau of stagnated growth.

- The pride of clinging to the way we have always done things. Past experience should be a guidepost, not a hitching post.

- The power play for control.

- Pulling down the walls of polarization.

- Pushing beyond the self-imposed walls of limitations.

- Propagating an abundance mentality in the place of a soup line mentality.

- Penetrating the community with the life transforming power of God.

Jesus was crucified as a Lamb but was resurrected as a Lion. *Turn the Lion loose.* He's never seen a problem that He could not solve, a disease He could not heal, a

| *Turn the Lion loose.* |

sin He could not forgive, a city He could not penetrate, or a marriage He could not salvage. Satan goes around "roaring" but the Lion of Judah goes about "PREVAILING."

Action Steps For God To Give You A Break Through.

Number 1, Confess your secret sins. (Isaiah 59:1-2) "Behold the Lord's hand is not shortened that it cannot save; neither his ear heave that it cannot hear, but YOUR iniquities have separated between you and your God, and your sins have hid his face from you that he will not answer." Sin must be confessed to be forgiven. (I John 1:9)

Number 2, Speak to your mountain. Name your mountain and call it by name commanding it to be removed and be cast into the sea and it shall be moved. (Mark 11:23)

Number 3, Settle your doubt problem. Mark 11:23 promises the mountains will obey your command if you doubt not.

Number 4, Stand firmly on the Word. You may tremble as you stand on the Rock of Ages, but the Rock will never tremble under you. I find the words of Priscilla Howe to be medicine for the faint hearted and share them with you. "Read the Bible to be wise, believe it to be safe, and practice it to be holy. It contains light to direct you, food to support you, and comfort to cheer you. It is the traveler's map, the pilgrim's staff, and the pilot's compass." And best of all, in Isaiah 55:11 God assures us that it will not return unto me void, but it shall accomplish that which I please, and it shall prosper in the thing whereto I sent it.

"God is faithful, who will not suffer you to be tempted above that you are able: but will with the temptation also make a way to escape, that ye may be able to bear it."
- God, ~ I Corinthians 10:13

"The true measure of a man is the height of his ideals, the breadth of his sympathy, the depth of his convictions, and the length of his patience."
-unknown-

God Got His Hands Dirty To Expose His Magnificence.

<u>Timeline</u>: 30 days before the revival is to begin.

Perspective: Three words describe the nature of God. HE WAS INVOLVED. He who owned the entire animal kingdom became dependent upon the hospitality of man to survive. As a babe, t, the Maker was more destitute than the men нe made. God had one Son that had no sin but could not say he had no sorrow. Hebrews 2:9 explains it so clearly. "But we see Jesus, who was made a little lower than the angels for the suffering of death, crowned with glory and honour; that he by the grace of God should taste death for every man." He who had servants in heaven came down here to serve; not to be served. He got his hands dirty to cleanse us from our sins.

By doing so, the offended judge became my Heavenly Father, and I—a guilty sinner—became His adopted son.

<u>Proposal</u>: Get involved. Abandon the routine. Do something different, and see what a difference God will make thru you.

Scripture Foundation:

"And as Jesus passed by, he saw a man which was blind from his birth. And his disciples asked him, saying, Master, who did sin, this man, or his parents, that he was born blind?

Jesus answered, Neither hath this man sinned, nor his parents:

but that the works of God should be made manifest in him...When he had thus spoken, he spat on the ground, and made clay of the spittle, and he anointed the eyes of the blind man with the clay, And said unto him, Go, wash in the pool of Siloam, (which is by interpretation, Sent.) He went his way therefore, and washed, and came seeing." (John 9:1-3, 6-7)

God created the vast, magnificent universe by the sound of His voice without any dirt on His hands, but He could not save one lost soul from sin without dirtying His hands on a rugged cross.

Jesus was not a prissy, pampered little brat from Paradise who was aloof and afraid to get involved in human lives. He made Mercury two fifths the size of the earth with a diameter of 3,032 miles. Mars is 33,900,000 miles from the earth at its closest distance and has a temperature that rarely rises above zero but can dip to as much as negative 87 degrees. He crafted the massive, magnificent universe lighting up the midnight sky with billions of stars, but He also made a mud pie.

Jesus was not a passive by-stander. He didn't have one passive bone in the 270 bones that He had at his birth nor one unsympathetic fiber in the 770,000 plus fibers of his optic nerve.

> *The Crowned Prince of heaven became homeless on earth so that the homeless on earth might have a home in heaven.*

The Crowned Prince of heaven became homeless on earth so that the homeless on earth might have a home in heaven.

He had callouses on His knees from prayer, splinters under His fingernails from working in a carpenter's shop, scales on His hands from cleaning fish, and red, blood shot eyes from weeping over Jerusalem; and His shoulders were raw from carrying His cross.

His Holiness was incontestable. His purpose in living and dying was pure. His conscience was clear. He was unblemished in character and spotless of sin. He was untarnished by vices and unsoiled by moral depravity, but He never hesitated to get His hands dirty when love and compassion demanded it.

Matthew recorded these highly significant words. "He (Jesus) was *moved* with compassion." (9:36) The Psalmist declared that God is *full* of compassion (86:15), and Jeremiah un-hesitantly proclaimed, "His compassions *fail not*." (Lamentations 3:22)

I have captured four separate instances in the life of Christ when His boundless compassion drove Him to get His immaculate hands dirty.

The first instance is when He dared tackle the problem of a man who was blind from the moment of his birth. I will refer to it as the moment He...

Reversed The Irreversible.

Jesus became a maverick and *a chance taker to expose the magnificence of God.* David Platt addressed this issue clearly when he declared, "I could not help but think that somewhere along the way we had missed what was radical about our faith and replaced it with what is comfortable."

Jesus broke the mold with His approach which was unconventional and probably disdained to the community at large. What he did was by no means politically correct. He made a mud pie, and smeared it on the eyes of the blind man. It probably offended the parents and infuriated the community, but it let God out of the box to show what He could do. He can reverse the irreversible and do the impossible.

I am afraid we are not radical enough to expect radical results. I challenge you to have and demonstrate: (1) a radical allegiance to your convictions; (2) a radical commitment to the mandates of our Lord and Master; (3) a radical courage to take action. Listen to "the still small voice" of God that is speaking to you now. Have the courage to leave your comfort zone and lodge your authority to act in the name of Jesus – cast off the yoke of bondage in worship, conciliate broken relationships, contend for the faith once delivered to the saints, call those things which art not as though they are, and celebrate in the glorious, victorious name of the Son of God.

Harold R. McAlindon said it like this. "Do not follow where the path may lead. Go instead where there is no path and leave a trail."

Jesus was a trailblazer. He declared, "I am the Way."

Jesus said, "If I be lifted up from the earth, will draw all men unto me." (John 12:32) If we deemphasize, demote Him, or still worse demonize the preaching of the Cross from our master plan for evangelism and church growth, *we have taken the magnetisms out of our ministry.* We become clouds without rain, trees without fruit, and ministries without miracles. (Jude 12) *When we dumb down the work of the Lion Tamer and expect to catch dinosaurs with a miniature mouse trap,* we shy away at the mention of revival. We must make Jesus the main attraction not a tag along has been. Unfortunately, over time, THE CHIEF CORNERSTON was and is being rejected. (Mark 12:10) It is critical for us to understand what the word reject means from the original language. *"Atheteo"* means to do away with. *"Atheton"* means without place. What a sobering absurdity. There was no place for Him at his birth and no prominent place for Him when He comes back again. This haunted Jesus when He asked, "Nevertheless when the Son of man cometh, shall he find faith on earth?" (Luke 18:8)

> *Lifting Jesus up is the essence of evangelism, the supreme purpose of His church and the magnetism that pulls men, women, boy and girls to an altar of regeneration and transformation.*

Lifting Jesus up is the essence of evangelism, the supreme purpose of His church, and the magnetisms that pulls men, women, boys, and girls to an altar of regeneration and transformation. If we genuinely want revival, we need to begin by pledging to lift up our Lord and Savior—Jesus Christ. He is the One:

- Who has all the resources of time and eternity to connect, convict, and convert the vilest of sinners? If it requires croaking frogs to cause Pharaoh to cave in; a rooster to reach the Big Fisherman in a place where preachers were not welcome…His capabilities are unlimited. O, dear men and women of God, we must lift him up when we have utilized all of our others methods and failed.

- He can deputize fish to make a special delivery to the disciples to pay their taxes. He can displace a star and guide it as a finger of light to point to the crib of the Savior. He can put words in the mouth of a dumb donkey to shock a man to his senses. He can stick a sack lunch in the beak of a big bird to make a home delivery to a prophet to keep him from starving to death. He can shake a jail at midnight to turn a jailer toward the saving grace of God. He can speak to the dead and when His words fall on those deaf ears the frozen blood in His veins thaws, and flows again. Lift Jesus up. He can make the impossibilities possible.

- He spoke from heaven to Saul of Tarsus, a proud, ruthless man who was leading a lynching party to commit murder or multiple murderers but was halted and blinded by a beaming light from heaven and heard a voice from another world shooting ripples through every steeled nerve in his body and wilted him like a cut flower in mid-day sun, until he cried, "What would you have me to do?" Lift him up. God got past his body guards and melted his stony heart. No one knew how to reach him, but God did.

- I borrow words from Anne Graham Lotz who reminded me again of why we must lift him up. "He seeks the strays; finds the lost; rights the wrongs; avenges the abused; he sympathizes with the hurting; he shields the helpless; mends the broken; and welcomes the prodigals." (end quote) O, brother and sister, lift him up. His grace is sufficient. His love is limitless. His Sovereignty has no shorelines. And His will is inviolable.

We must get involved and lift Jesus up whatever it takes. Revival or spiritual renewal must not be as out dated as a Model T Ford or as extinct as a Himalayan dinosaur.

Jude graphically describes what it means to get involved in reaching the lost as "pulling them out of the fire." (v. 22) That means feeling the heat, getting the smell of smoke in your clothes, soot in your eyes, blisters and charcoal on your hands, and inhalation of sweltering heat. It means running risks before reaping a reward.

Secondly, He got his hands dirty when he chose to show...

Love To The Unlovable

Jesus came on a mission to love everyone even the unlovable, the down and out, as well as the rich and famous. Paul described his unmeasurable humiliation by so doing in these simple but illustrative words in Philippians 2:6-8. "Who being in the form of God, thought it not robbery to be equal with God: But made himself of no reputation, and took upon him the form of a servant, and was made in the likeness of men: And being found in in fashion as a man, he humbled himself, and became obedient unto death, even the death of the cross."

Almighty God could not get any lower. The Darling of the glory world took upon Himself the form of a servant. It was His choice. He could have been a *Michelangelo* in art and architecture; a *Galileo* of astronomy and physics; a *Handel* in composing musical scores; a *Jonas Salk* to bring the world a vaccine to cure a dreaded disease; or *Albert Einstein*, the most famous scientist of the 20th century, who changed how we view our world.

"But he made himself," the Bible declares. He made himself a God who was willing to dirty His hands in an effort to transcend linguistic, cultural, and geographic boundaries and change the eternal destinies of all human kind.

Jesus did the unthinkable when he came the unknown distance from mansions in the sky to a desolate manger in Bethlehem to drape a rainbow of hope around the world.

Omnipotence was reduced to the impotent biceps of an infant's tiny arms.

Omnipotence was reduced to the impotent biceps of an infant's tiny arms. Omniscience was limited in thought to a little baby crying to find the breast of His mother to satisfy his hunger. And I might add, *Omnipresence* was confined to the four walls of a smelly barn where vermin raced about on the mud floor.

At His birth, dirt was under His crib, and in His ministry mud was on His hands. The entire episode of "God becoming man" was an unthinkable surprise. It was a good thing that a bright, shining star led the Wise Men to the Bethlehem manger where the new born King was found. Speaking in modern terms, they would have never imagined that they would find God curled up in a bed of straw in an outhouse.

They, like Elijah, might look for God in the roar of rumbling thunder, or clothed with the lightning flashing across the sky, or somewhere in the wake of a howling whirlwind, but never in the backyard of a quaint bed and breakfast motel. Perhaps in Taj Mahal, the famous mausoleum of India, or Coliseum of Italy which is the largest amphitheater in the world, or the Eiffel tower in France, or the Hanging Gardens of Babylon.

But on one occasion they found Him sitting on the floor with his feet and legs curled under Him like a pretzel dirtying His hands washing and drying feet. This was not an elected position. It was a voluntary choice. No one else wanted the job. This was the lowest position in the house. It was on the floor. No one could look up but down on him.

The question is not where can I find God? The real question is – where can God <u>not</u> be found? God can be found on the floor cleaning dirt from under toe nails. It was a most unlikely place for a Celestial Dignitary. The Psalmist dealt with the same question and answered it. "Whither shall I go from thy spirit? or whither shall I flee from thy presence? If I ascend up into heaven, thou art there: if I make my bed in hell, behold, thou art there. If I take the wings of the morning, and dwell in the uttermost parts of the sea; Even there shall thy hand lead me, and thy right hand shall hold me. If I say, Surely the darkness shall cover me; even the night shall be light about me." (Palms 139:7-11) In Proverbs 15:3 we are assured that "the eyes of the Lord are in every place."

God knows all, sees all, and hears all when we pray.

This means that we may have a revolutionary rendezvous with God in some very unlikely places.

- Eating fresh corn on the cob in the field on the Sabbath. (Mark 2:23-24)

- Looking up in a tree and talking to a man who is straddling a limb. (Luke 19:1-6)

- Making a house call to see a sick woman.(Matthew 14-15)

- Talking to a dead man at the mouth of a tomb. (John 11:37-44)

- A cattle shed in Bethlehem. (Luke 2:16)

- Hanging out with the guys on a boat dock. (John 21:3-12)

- Getting saw dust in his hair at this dad's carpenter shop. (Mark 6:3)

- On a mountain climbing outing. (Matthew 17:1)

- Shackled and under heavy guard in jail. (Acts 16:22-27)

- In Kangaroo court standing up for the accused. (John 8:3-11)

- Bethesda pool side gathering. (John 5:2-8)

- Fish fry on the sea shore. (John 21:9)

- Wedding in Cana of Galilee. (John 2:9)

- Gathering wood for a camp fire. (Acts 28:1-5)

- Riding a donkey in a parade in Jerusalem. (Matthew 21:2-9)

- Teaching at a house church in Capernaum. (Mark 1-2)

- Sitting down to chat with a woman at the town's watering hole. (John 4:6-29)

- Falling asleep in a fishing boat. (Matthew 23-26)

- Jumping in a fiery furnace to visit his Hebrew buddies who were in trouble. (Daniel 3:19-25)
- A dying thug hanging on a bloody cross with one foot in the grave. (Luke 23:39-43)
- My mom found Him in an outhouse.
- I found him in a little, country farm house.

The conclusion is simple. Anyone can find God anywhere and at any time. I know, I discovered that when I was willing to get my hands and shoes dirty. I'll not go into details that lead up to this incredible adventure I had beside the railroad track. When I arrived two winos were slouched on a bench under the shade. I introduced myself and asked them if we could have a little church service with them. They could have cared less, so I began. It was nuts to expect these red faced, bleary eyed hobos to stay awake long enough to know where they were and what we were doing. But we sang a little and I brought them a message about Jesus and his love. My job was done, and I started to leave. But a little, small voice reminded me that I had forgotten something. Like what? Like, "Would you like to accept Jesus and have forgiveness of sin?

I knew that still, small voice. I reluctantly obeyed by asking them if they would like to accept Jesus and pray? I struggled to imagine that they knew who Jesus was, what forgiveness meant, and if it registered to them at all. I am sorry to admit it, but I was surprised to see one of them lift his hand. 50% of my congregation responded to the simple invitation. We prayed together, and he accepted Jesus as his Savior and Lord. I believe angels were rejoicing in heaven. As I got my hands and shoes dirty, he got a clean heart with God. Then my shocker came when he told me who he was. This wino was a preacher's kid who went wrong. He wanted to get his life straightened out and needed the help of God. He found it in an unlikely place—on a makeshift bench beside a railroad track.

> *This wine-o was a preacher's kid who went bad, and found God in an unlikely place on a makeshift bench beside a railroad track.*

God turned that place into a cathedral that I will never forget.

I know what you are thinking, but you are wrong. Five years passed before I saw him again. It was in a restaurant in Little Rock, Arkansas. He came to our table and apologized for the interruption but wanted me to know who he was. The man who accepted Jesus by the railroad track joyfully reported that he had been sober for 5 years and living for God. Who knows what God will do if you are willing to get your hands dirty?

It reminds me so much of a sign hanging from the wall of a public historical site which read: "What is past is Prologue." When an inquisitive visitor asked, "What does it mean?" The guide quickly replied, "You ain't seen nothing yet."

The God who became man died with dirty hands. Look at them closely as He died on the cross. They were nail pierced and dripping with blood. He died with dirty hands to crowd heaven with men and women who have clean hearts through the blood of the precious Redeemer.

YOU AIN'T SEEN NOTHING YET. Turn him loose in your town and see what he will do.

Action Steps: Be filled with the Spirit

- CONSIDER what being filled with the Spirit means (Ephesians 5:18-20; 3:19; Colossians 1:9; John 15:11)
- COMMIT your life to the purpose of being filled with all the fullness of God. (Ephesians 3:16 – 20; 5:18)
- CELEBRATE the life and liberty that comes with being filled with all the fullness of God.

Celebrate joyfully, enthusiastically, spontaneously, and victoriously.

"Anyone can become angry. That is easy, but to be angry with the right person and to the right degree and at the right time and for the right purpose and in the right way is not easy."

-Aristotle-

Be Just Like Jesus: Get Mad At The Devil

<u>Fighting for revival</u>

<u>Time line</u>: NOW!

<u>Perspective</u>: No matter how hard we try, we can never be neutral. Jesus was never neutral when dealing with the devil. He got so mad for what the devil has done to our world that He died to break his hold on the human race. He didn't come to diplomatically try to find common grounds for Heaven and Hell to live side by side in peace. No. He came to destroy the devil and his demonic forces.

<u>Proposal</u>: Get mad at the devil every time you pass by a mortuary, hear of a drive by shooting, read someone committed suicide, see the pain of divorce, know about a church split, or be asked to pray for someone who is dying of cancer, etc. These things are delivered to humanity with the devil's signature one them.

Scripture Foundation:

"Jesus found the Temple teeming with people selling cattle and sheep and doves. The loan sharks were also there in full strength. Jesus put together a whip out of strips of leather and chased them out of the Temple...upending the tables of the loan sharks, spilling coins left and right. He told the dove merchants, Get your things out of here. Stop turning my Father's house into a shopping mall. That's when his disciples remembered the Scripture, Zeal for your house consumes me." (John 2:14-17 – The Message)

Ever since I was a freckled face kid, I was taught to do my best to be like Jesus. It meant to love as He loved, obey as He obeyed, serve as He served, pray as He prayed and be holy as He is holy. Scholars tell us that Ephesians 5:1 literally means to be "imitators" of God. That was drilled into me, *but no one ever suggested that if I was to be like Jesus, I should get mad and stay mad at the devil because Jesus did.*

The text we just read paints the picture of an angry God lashing out at Beelzebub (Matthew 12:24) which means lord of the fly. Flies contaminate everything they touch. The "fly" was at work in the church attempting to corrupt, pervert, and out right destroy all that he came in contact with.

When Jesus saw "the fly" at work misusing and abusing the Father's House, He blew up.

God's glory moved out when the money changers moved in.

It was a sacred place to him, but entrepreneurs converted it into a shopping mall. Capitalist went there for business, but God intended His house to be a house of prayer and rendezvous with Him.

The altar, in essence, was to be a designated meeting place with God, but crafty sales pros converted it into a yard sale profit center. What a happy hunting ground for venders who peddle their goods to a built-in network of friends who attend the same church and did not expect anyone to pick their pockets or be scammed.

Money changers squeezed out the life changers, and God's glory moved out when the money changers moved in. *God's House was under new management* and the light house was beginning to grow dim.

I tried to relate it to my own children. What if they came to my house, and when they came inside they discovered that squatters had taken over, driven me out, and they found:

- The living room had used clothing stacked to the ceiling for a garage sale.

- The bed room was a brothel to accommodate the depraved sex trade.
- The bath room was a meth lab.
- The library was a promo and sales lounge for pornography.
- The garage was an oily, greasy auto parts store used asa cover for drug dealers.
- And the kitchen was a modern-day chat room for pimps to pilfer.

In my wildest imagination, I cannot envision my kids walking in calmly and politely, examining the house room by room, smiling mildly, and simply saying, "Well, it was never like this when my father lived here. I am sure that he would be disappointed, but it is what it is, so let's live and let live. Have a great day."

Oh no. If it was my house, they would rip, snort, and roar, and the gates of hell would be trembling in terror. They would implement an immediate **hostile** take over, and hostile would be the proper word. Don't mess with my father's house or you will have to answer to his loving kids.

> *Don't mess with my Father's House or you will answer to his loving kids.*

That's essentially what Jesus told Pilate. In John 18:36, he assured Pilate that if my kingdom were of this world, then would my servants fight that I should not be delivered to the Jews.

The children of the King must not roll over and play dead when the adversary is rolling his sleeves up and taking advantage of every opportunity to harass, embarrass, out class, and out last children of the Most High God.

We are not called to be wall flowers and baby sitters. We are called to be warriors to wage war on the enemies of the Cross and soldiers who will go to battle to win for the

> *The enemies of the cross should be shaking in their boots when the Kids of the King rise up to confront any and every foe of the Cross and Crucified.*

cause of Christ. The enemies of the cross (Philippians 3:18) should be shaking in their boots when the Kids of the King rise up to confront any and every foe of the Cross and Crucified. Goliath could not believe that a lad hardly old enough to shave would dare venture into his pathway. But David was ready to fight for the honor of God.

Paul was a fighter and issued this injunction to every believer in I Timothy 6:12. "Fight the good fight…" This warrior testified at the close of his life, I have fought a good fight; I have finished my course, I have kept the faith. (II Timothy 4:7)

Paul further declares that "the effeminate" will not inherit the kingdom of God. (I Corinthians 6:9) The word effeminate means to be soft.

This is not a time for the Church to go soft. We must not go down in history as the church of timidity but the Church triumphant fighting for:

> *We must not go down in history as the church of timidity but the Church triumphant.*

- ✓ The inerrancy of Scripture.
- ✓ Indispensability of the birth, life, death, resurrection, and ascension of Jesus Christ.
- ✓ Intolerance of sin and inborn love for sinners.
- ✓ Inexhaustibility of God's love.
- ✓ Inevitability of judgment.
- ✓ Insidious reality of the person and work of the devil.
- ✓ Intrinsic nature of God to hear and answer prayer.
- ✓ Invincible power of God to send revival regardless of adverse circumstances.

We must fight. We must win. We have no other choice. If we don't fight, the enemy will win by default. I am challenged heavily by the words of Dante Alighieri who insisted that "the hottest places in hell are reserved for those who in time of moral crisis preserved their neutrality." Charles Schumer also had strong words for the softies when he wrote, "Inaction is perhaps the greatest mistake of all."

Jesus got MAD and came out fighting not looking like the Gentle Shepherd but more like the Lion of the tribe of Judah. His mild manner took a sudden and unexpected turn. He took all He could take and exploded. Look at Him carefully. It was not a docile, soft spoken Messenger from mansions in the sky that manned a whip, kicked over tables, sent cattle stampeding, and demanding that the guilty offenders get out of the house of God.

Perhaps we are not angry enough by what we see in our cities and world as Jesus was, but we should be. Children are the innocent prey of pedophiles. Homes are being mangled by moral malignancy. Religious institutions are gutted by political correctness rather than guided by the precedence of Scripture. The truth is irrelevant. Holiness is an antiquated term that has gone out of style. Illicit sex has the stamp of approval from Hollywood. The cancer of theological apostasy is eating the soul out of evangelism. 500,000 kids attempt suicide every year and 6,000 succeed.

If this won't make your blood boil, I don't know what could.

It makes me mad when I realize that what R.T. Ketcham said is true in many cases. "(they) prefer science to Scripture, reason for revelation, benevolence for blood, goodness for grace, sociability for spirituality, play for praise, progress for power, feeling for faith, politics for precepts and pep for prayer."

I am angry enough to turn my anger against the devil and his devious plans for you, your family, and your church. Let me count the ways.

- He promotes the spirit of disobedience and fills us with misinformation concerning God. (Genesis 3:4)
- He is a liar and father of all lies. (John 8:44)
- His mission is to devour beautiful and precious things. (I Peter 5:8)
- He is a habitual thief, a heartless killer, and takes pleasure in destroying everything in his pathway. (John 10:10)

- He blinds people to the light of the glorious, good news of the gospel. (II Corinthians 4:3-4)

- He, when permitted by God, does all sorts of bad things to good people. (Job 1:9)

- He is a ruthless murderer. (John 8:44)

- He preys on the innocent, and shoots arrows into the heart of hope.

- He is the ruler of darkness and releases demonic presence at will. (Ephesians 6:12)

- He has the audacity to attempt to outsmart God. (Matthew 4:1)

- He dares to confront angels. (Zechariah 3:1)

- He has power to possess human beings and pigs go crazy when under his control. (Luke 9:42, Mark 5:13)

When I understand who the devil is and what he does, I fully understand why Ephesians 4:27 admonishes us to avoid giving the devil one inch.

Give him a social drink and he will demand a 6-pack; give him a sneak peek of pornography and he will drag you into addiction; give him a seed of discord in church, and he will dismantle it piece by piece; give him a taste of control in a church or denomination, and he will develop control freaks.

Don't give the devil an inch, no place to linger or dwell. Only a person who is out of their mind would take a:

- ✓ known rapist, invite him to stay in their home with only a 6 inch wall between him and their beautiful daughter.

- ✓ take a habitual thief and give him the code to your personal safe.

- ✓ trust a sociopath with a room full of guns and knives and a can of cyanide sitting on the shelf.

- ✓ pick up a hitch-hiker in middle of the night with a K-16 hanging on his shoulder and an automatic 45 strapped to his belt.

✓ Give a drug addict a credit card and actually expect him to use it sparingly and wisely.

That's the problem. He doesn't show up looking like a rapist, sociopath, or a ruthless murderer. The Bible tells us that he represents himself as an "angel of light." (II Corinthians 11:14)

We get fooled by what appears to be an angel, someone to be trusted, helpful, and may be an answer to prayer. But he has the heart of a terrorist and mindset of a monster.

Jesus had these strong words of warning to each of us. "Watch therefore: for ye know not what hour your Lord doth come. But know this, that if the goodman of the house had known in what watch the thief would come, he would have watched, and would not have suffered his house to be broken up." (Matthew 24:42-43)

We must direct our anger at the source of our problems— the devil. He's devious and destructive; mad and mean. He walks abouttaking his time:

- to erode your happiness;
- infiltrate your marriage;
- persuade your children to turn from God by peer pressure;
- to make evil look good and good evil;
- to melt resistance to moral purity by an avalanche of bill board and television magic;
- and pins a happy face on pimps and drug lords.

He's the king of gossip, mayor of misery, lord of lusts, admiral of abominations, general of greed, chief of charlatans, commander of demonic activity; director of moral rot; emperor of confusion and discontent; dictator of doubt; ring leader of corruption in the church; the engineer of all works of evil; overseer of the overtures to minimize the power in the Blood of the Lord Jesus Christ; superintendent of a demolition crew whose purpose is to crucify Christ all over again, curse and defy the God of heaven, crush his church, and would like nothing better than to cancel the return of the Lord Jesus Christ.

A protracted meeting will do nothing to confront and conquer this enemy. Protracted meetings and revivals are not one and the same. Protracted meetings open the doors at the appointed time for people to come in, but never seem to get the doors open for God to come in. The frigid winds of formality blow, but the rushing, mighty wind of the Holy Spirit are painfully absent. True revival turns the light of the Gospel on in the kingdom of darkness, robs hell, populates heaven, and wages war against the devil. True revival shakes slumbering saints out of their sleep, lights fire in worship, infuses power into prayers, and breaks chains of bondage.

> *True revival turns the light of the Gospel on in the kingdom of darkness, robe hell, populates heaven, and wages war against the devil.*

Action Steps

Look for an open door to do something for Jesus (Revelation 3:8 "set before you an open door"). Remember Jesus ministered to a man straddled a limb up a tree.

I found that opportunity to minister to a man sprawled out under a tree beside the road. It all started when I looked out the window of my office and saw the town drunk staggering along and alone down the side of a street. Without preplanning, it was like I was pulled out of my office chair and pushed toward the outside door. I caught myself running toward him.

He was startled when he heard my voice and was really startled when I reached him saying, "Just wanted you to know that I love you and God loves you too." I got this funny look accompanied by this question. "What did you say, honey?" Then he continued, "Nobody has told me they loved me since I was a little boy."

We had a revival under an oak tree, sitting on green grass as all heaven must have been on tip toes and broke out with song when he accepted Jesus. He was in church the following weekend wearing his "Sunday go to meetin'" best. I don't know where he is now, but I hope he is in heaven because I found an open door under an old, oak tree.

Start looking for open doors in:

- Unlikely places—car wash, beauty salon, grocery store, ball game, etc.
- Unplanned meetings that are not accidental.
- Unknown individuals that God brings across your pathway.
- Unfortunate people who need your help.
- Unrealized avenues to serve Christ in your church.

<u>Learn</u> life lessons that will change your life forever (Revelation 5:5 "weep not"). Please read and re-read over and over again. Read it until it is tattooed in our spirit.

- Things are not always as bad as they seem to be. (Revelation 5:5 - weep not...the Lion has prevailed)
- God knows and understands what you have gone through and appreciates it more than you may realize He does. (Revelations 3:8 - I know thy works...you have little strength and have kept my word, and have not denied my name.)
- God has keys to open and shut doors at his will that man cannot undo or redo. (Revelation 3:7-8 – He has the key of David...He opens, and no man shuts; and shuts and no man opens.)
- God has keeping power regardless of the storms that come. (Revelation 3:10 – "I will also keep you...")

<u>Lift</u> your eyes toward the Throne of God. (Revelation 5:6 – "And I beheld...") Pay close attention to the things He discovered when He was looking in the right direction.

- He discovered that God was still on His Throne. (v. 7)
- He discovered that Jesus is indispensable in time and eternity. (v. 5)
- He discovered that prayers are carefully preserved in heaven. (v. 8)
- He discovered that God has made us kings and priests,

and we shall reign on earth. (v. 10)

- He discovered that worship and praise will probably be loud in heaven. (v. 12)
- He discovered that Jesus is alive and well. (v.1)

God's time for revival is the very darkest hour, when everything seems hopeless. It is always the Lord's way to go to the very worst cases to manifest His glory.
- Andrew Gih-

*May the dreams of your past
be the reality of your future.*
-Author unknown-

Back To The Future
(Revival - Then And Now)

Timeline: 30 to 60 days <u>before</u> revival start date.

Prospective on revival: The concepts of revival are old, but the need is ever new.

Proposal: Read this paper with an open mind and heart. Jesus said, He that hath an ear, let him hear what the Spirit is saying to the churches. (Revelation 2:7, 11, 17, 29; 3:6, 13, 22)

Back to the future is a term which has come to be used to simply mean going back to a past practice in the present. Too many yesterdays are kisses dried up on our cheeks, ice cream that is melted, coke that has lost its fizz, and eagles without wings. In other words, they consider revivals to have lost their excitement, be unappealing at best, and they don't fly in this generation. But they're treasures from the past that are far more than trinkets to trivialize or motivators to modernize.

Miracles are back to the future moments when Eden's glory is temporarily restored. Jurgen Moltmann proclaimed, "Jesus's healings are not supernatural miracles in a natural world. They are the only truly 'natural' things in a world that is

> *Miracles are back to the future moments when Eden's glory is temporarily restored.*

unnatural, demonized, and wounded." Revivals are such moments.

Since I have not only heard about revival and been impacted by revival, I can personally attest to the unquestionable value they have had on my life. Without controversy, we need to reach back into the past and reestablish...

1. Celebratory praise and worship.

2. Intense prayer time kneeling at an altar.

3. Preaching and preachers that are heavily anointed by the Holy Spirit.

4. High, eager anticipation of what God will do here and now.

5. Sacred interruptions of the Holy Spirit when man relinquishes his control over to God's control.

6. Unfettered joy.

7. Timer turned off and triumph turned on.

Please don't start trash talking or ramble on about adjusting to a more seeker friendly programing. Let me remind you that times have changed but somethings haven't.

- Human nature has not changed.

- The devil hasn't changed in character and purpose.

- The need for a divine visitation has not waned.

- The reality of the rapture has not changed.

- The demand for holy living has not changed.

- The Judge and coming judgment we must all face have not changed.

- The purpose of the crucifixion of Jesus has not been suspended or amended.

- Jesus hasn't changed nor has the purpose and need for revival.

Robert Coleman defined revival as: "that sovereign work of God in which He visits His own people, restoring

> *Revival is much ado about nothing until the glory comes.*

and releasing them into the fullness of His blessing." It is a one on one encounter with God. No, it is not a church growth extravaganza, but I will submit that a genuine revival will grow THE church. As a matter of fact, revival is much ado about nothing until the glory comes.

Webster's Revised Unabridged Dictionary defines revive as: 1. To return to life; to recover life or strength; to live anew; to become reanimated or reinvigorated. 2. Hence, to recover from a state of oblivion, obscurity, neglect, or depression; 3. To restore, or bring again to life; to reanimate. 4. To raise from coma, languor, depression, or discouragement; to bring into action after a suspension.

Spurgeon explained revive like this. "The word "revive" wears its meaning upon its forehead; it is from the Latin, and may be interpreted thus—to live again, to receive again a life which has almost expired; to rekindle into a flame the vital spark which was nearly extinguished."

I love these words of Nancy Leigh DeMoss. "Revival is not just an emotional touch; it's a complete takeover!" Duncan Campbell must have had a tongue anointed by God when he proclaimed that revival is *"a community saturated with God."*

It is a God consciousness and a total abandon with Him. It's not showmanship or artistry or counterfeit representations of the Glory of God. It's when the glory world bends down to touch our world, and we get a taste of that world. It's falling in love with Jesus all over again. It carries me back

> *Revival is falling in love with God all over again.*

to the first love fascination and excitement with Jesus and brings it back to the future—now. It is a world changer in my Christian walk. In those moments, I...

1. Recognize the presence of sin and repent.

2. Restore spontaneity in worship.

3. Rediscover the awesome nature of God.

4. Repair broken relationships.

5. Recapture unadulterated love for Jesus.

6. Redouble our efforts to reach the lost.

7. Release God's power to work in and thru us. It puts new emphasis on signs and wonders, and de-emphasizes positions of power to demand demonstrations of power.

America needs such a spiritual awakening. The Church needs a shaking. The economy needs fixing. Uptight, stressed out believers need an unwinding. The devil and his cohorts need a binding. This all adds up to one thing. We need a mind boggling, heart throbbing, soul transforming, and city moving visitation of God.

There are some great and mighty things that money can't buy and schools can't franchise. It's God jumping out of the box when He gets so disgusted with profiteers who know it all, and God blows the lid off and shows up in his power and great glory. It's that moment when God wakes up the sleeping, fires up the lukewarm, cheers up the disgruntled, shuts up the gossipers, and opens up the windows of heaven and pours out blessings which we can't contain. He rebukes the devourer, resuscitates hope, removes sin, reconciles the estranged, and restores joy. I cast my vote for and call upon our God who not only knows all but can do all things according to his promises. God will show up and when he does he will show off for his people!

I pray that you and your church will have a "*divine discontentment seizure*" as did 4 lepers (II Kings 7:1-3) that muttered 7 words to each other that turned their world right side up. Those 7, simple words were, "WHY SIT WE HERE TILL WE DIE?" They had a

> *They had a supernatural discontentment seizure for living as underprivileged and rose up to claim privileges that were almost within their reach but never realized.*

seizure of super discontentment for living as underprivileged and rose up to claim privileges that were almost within their reach but never realized.

Their discontentment was the antecedent of change. Florence Nightingale explained the mystical power of discontentment like this. "Were there none who were discontented with what they have, the world would never reach anything better." Dr. Charles Stanley described how discontentment can move us from striving to thriving in life when he wrote, "Believers…become discontent with "surviving" and have taken the time to investigate everything God has to offer in this life."

> *Discontentment is the antecedent of change.*

The 4 lepers in our text were motivated by discontentment to take matters into their own hands and do something about it. Doing nothing was suicidal and the kiss of death. As I am writing this message, a picture suddenly flashed on the mirror of my mind of a revival I was preaching in my early days of ministry. It was a small church, and I must admit that this particular service was about as dull, boring, and unexciting as watching the grass grow on the lawn. It was almost past sucking the oxygen out of an oxygen tank to keep alive until we could all rush out and go home. I will never forget my text. "Why sit we here till we die?" Couldn't have been more current and appropriate, but while I labored to get through it, a little, elderly lady sitting in the middle row simply raised her hand toward God and begin to praise Him, and she received an incredible gift from God.

She didn't tell me this, but in my mind, I imagine she was saying, "Why sit we here till we die?" In her discontent, she made a faith dash to God and landed in a net of God's grace.

That's exactly what the lepers did. There are 4 admirable characteristics of these men that evolved from 7 simple words "Why sit we here till we die" that catapulted them into what I will call their revival.

> *She made a faith dash to God and landed in the net of God's grace.*

First Of All, They Were <u>Fanatics</u>.

They were not movers and shakers as we know it today. They were health hazards to their community, displaced to an isolated colony of people who were terminally ill with incurable leprosy and left alone to live and die there. *But they believed they could go where they had been told they shouldn't and reaped benefits they were assured they wouldn't.*

They were lepers and had no right to enter certain forbidden zones and enjoy privileges that others had, but fanatics don't follow the stogie old rules and abide by public policies.

> *Fanatics have a radicalized relationship with God that does not subside, a headstrong faith and wild expectations from the resurrected Lord.*

Fanatics tear roofs off to get a crippled man to Jesus, build boats with no place to sail it, challenge giants with a sling shot, sing and praise God at midnight in jail with chains hanging from their ankles, hang a scarlet thread out from their window and fully expect to be protected from vigilantes. They have a radicalized relationship with God, a domineering devotion that does not subside, headstrong faith, and wild expectations from the resurrected Lord. They believe the unbelievable and think the unthinkable. Fanatics refuse to settle for little when God promised them much. A fanatic will follow the lead of Jacob who cried out with a loud voice, I will not let you go until you bless me. (Genesis 32:26)

- ✓ Fanatics ignore the rules to reap rewards.
- ✓ Fanatics get tired of living in ruts and break out.
- ✓ Fanatics are ordinary people who walk with and believe in an extraordinary God.
- ✓ Fanatics never give up, but exercise the right to try all over again.
- ✓ Fanatics are ever optimistic.
- ✓ Fanatics fully subscribe to Goethe who said, "Things which matter most must never be at the mercy of thing which matter least." Jesus said, " But seek ye first the kingdom of God, and his righteousness; and all these things shall be added unto you." (Matthew 6:33) Fanatics put God first and other things to follow.

Secondly, The 4 Men Were <u>Forward</u>.

They were hardly considered to be the most likely to succeed, but they didn't believe it. The Bible describes such men as "bold as a lion." (Proverbs 28:1) They meet the prophets of Baal on a hillside for a prayer-o-thon and call a fire ball down from heaven. We must be bold and tenacious, and stand up and demand the release of spiritual gifts; order the adversary to release our sons and daughters from the bondage of sin; oppose quenching and grieving the Spirit, and take back what the enemy has stolen from us.

John Knox cried out to God. "Give me Scotland or I die."

Where or what is your Scotland that needs a revival? We need to become mountain talkers, devil stalkers, and noisemakers.

We need to become mountain talkers, devil stalkers, and noisemakers. Jesus commanded us to say unto this mountain, be thou removed and be thou cast into the sea (Mark 11:23).

The Bible tells us to put on the whole armor of God that you man be able to stand against the wiles of the devil. (Ephesians 6:11) We are further commanded to resist the devil, and he will flee from you. (James 4:7) In Psalms 47:1 we are commanded "to clap our hands…shout unto God with the voice of triumph. For the Lord most high is (awesome); he is a great King over all the earth. He shall subdue the people under us, and the nations under our feet."

Forward preachers will be aggressive in seeking a genuine revival not retreating. We must speak with the voice of authority, pray with executive privilege, preach as a mouth piece of God, prophecy boldly, and actively release signs and wonders according to what a believer has been promised. (Mark 16:17)

We must believe that Heaven is not in adjournment, the Throne of Grace is not temporarily out of order, and miracles haven't been suspended until further notice.

We must be the light shining in the darkness, the voice crying in the wilderness and the ambassador of the Almighty.

> *A revival is the Maker at work doing whatever He can, wherever He can with everything He has at His command.*

This is the time for us to come "BOLDLY to the throne of grace…" and confidently to the Maker who gave a donkey a tongue to talk, stars arrows to fight, iron buoyancy to float, and bushes that caught on fire, defied the laws of conflagration, and refused to burn up.

A revival is the Maker at work doing whatever He can wherever He can with everything He has at His command.

The Third Characteristic That These Men Had Is: They Were <u>Fearless</u>.

They had no idea what they would face when they entered the gates of the enemy. They were at the gate of plenty but not in it. They were close and yet so far from having their heart's desire.

This was a new experience to them which they had never tried to do before. It demanded fearlessness to enter the forbidden zone and walk past the off limits sign to discover a miracle.

We face the same fears today as we take aim on revival.

1. The fear of the <u>unknown</u> is one each of us must overcome. Peter must have thought about the unknown when he stepped out of his safety zone to walk on water. The disciples no doubt stumbled over the unknowns when they told Jesus that the tax bill was due and they had no money. What was His response? "Let's go fishing." This was no sick joke or blind denial of reality. No. Jesus knew the end from the beginning and everything in between. There comes a moment when we must commit the unknown future to our known God.

The fear of the <u>untried</u> is a second obstacle to vault over. We are victims of "that's not the way we do it." These lepers had probably never tried to sneak in the back door for a miracle. They never tried to see what would happen if they ventured into a new territory. Noah had never tried building a ship before.

> *Jesus knows the end from the beginning and everything in between.*

Moses had never tried throwing a dried, twisted stick on the ground to see it turn into a snake and then catch it by the tail. It was all new to him, but it worked when he obeyed God. God told one man He was going to do a new thing. That meant it had never been tried before, but it was safe to do because God was in it.

Between you and God, you can expect to see the impossible take place that everyone else said was improbable.

2. And there is the fear of an <u>uncertain</u> outcome which paralyzes any action at all. Billy Sills made a statement that challenges me to try even if the outcome is uncertain. He said, "You may be disappointed if you fail, but you are doomed if you don't try." Wayne Gretzky, the legendary hockey player, put it this way. "You miss 100% of the shots you don't take."

Joshua took a shot that was amazingly bold when he challenged the children of God to cross the flooding, dangerous river, and possess the Promised Land. It looked impossible, but isn't that the assignment of every pastor and minister? Isn't it our job to lead people to believe and accept the promises of God? However, it is from this dubious position that we struggle with numerous "What if's." "What if's" must have bounced around in Joshua's head like a ping pong ball. "What if" the priest were swept off their feet when they stepped into the churning water? "What if" the Ark of the Covenant slipped off the shoulder of the priest and crashed and was carried off in splintered pieces as the flood waters raged never to be seen again? "What if" the floods increased and the army of God got washed away and drowned in the violent water? Or "what if" the priest used conventional wisdom and refused to step into the water for fear of being washed away?

That is the negative "what if" side, but we forget the most important "what if" of all. "What if" God ignores the rational of human logic? "What if" God sets aside the laws of nature temporarily? "What if" invisible walls form a tunnel to hold waters at bay? "What if" the people walk through the tunnel on dry ground and possess the Promised Land and no one gets muddy feet or drowns?

I must ask myself – "what if" God shows up in all his power and glory? That's exactly what happened in Matthew 21:5. Jesus was in the house. Jesus makes the difference. When He is missing and adventure is gone from attending the house of God, we resort to worldly methods to generate crowds. We bribe or bait people to come. We don't call it that. We call it promotions or good marketing, but we offer prizes or a bonus for just showing up. Instead of using God's methods, we compensate by gimmicks, gadgets, and side show performances.

Jesus takes uncertainties out of the formula. A blind man did not come to a service that Jesus was conducting hoping to get a Seeing Eye Dog. That would have

> *Jesus brings adventure back into worship and attending church.*

given him happy feet, but he would have still had blind eyes. He came with great excitement and expectations to receive his sight and was not disappointed.

Jesus brings adventure back into worship and attending church. *I can walk down the aisle of the church and whisper* – Jesus is here and nothing is impossible. *Jesus is here* and miracles are a rule with him, not an occasional exception. *Jesus is here* and mercy and grace are flowing freely. *Jesus is here* and he is undaunted, undismayed, and unafraid of any adversaries, assailants, or anything else that may be annoying me. *Jesus is here* to cure diseases, conquer fear and cast away my sins. *Jesus is here. Let the adventures begin.*

We minimize what that really means. Daniel in a furnace with flames leaping around his body could say, "Jesus is here" and not get burned. Whatever you are facing, begin to say Jesus is here and has prepared stepping stones to hope for today and a brighter tomorrow. Jesus is here to mediate for my transgressions and provide for my forgiveness. Jesus is here and the doom of despair is dispelled by the dawn created by the Bright and Morning Star.

In our dying moment, we can triumphantly declare, "Jesus is here. I will not walk through the valley of the shadow of death alone."

I can't drop this ball and fumble this opportunity to shout into our world of uncertainties Jesus IS HERE in His Lordship to control, in His Headship to command, in His Heirship to bestow blessings untold, and in His Kingship to comfort us with kingdom privileges. We cannot be certain of the process, but we can be certain of the outcome because Jesus Christ is Lord.

The Fourth Characteristic Of The 4 Lepers Is: They Were <u>Focused</u>.

Focus and faith are the two eyes of vision that see what's possible and what's coming before it gets here.

> *Focus and faith are the two eyes of vision that sees what's possible and coming before it gets here.*

It's Elijah encouraging the king to put on a raincoat and rubber boots and run for shelter when there was only a small cloud floating in the sky.

It's Jesus telling a famished multitude to sit down for a picnic knowing that they only had a little guy's sack lunch to share. It's the God Man telling the distraught disciples that Lazarus was not dead but sleeping and went to wake him up from the deep slumber of death. He saw the end from the beginning and everything in between.

Don't be distracted. Stay focused on Him who is not frightened by any foe, subdued by any supplanter, unnerved by unbelievers, and overcome by countless obstacles. He succeeded in calming the churning waters of the sea, subjugating demons to cower to his command, and dominating diseases.

Focus on Jesus who is undaunted by the devil's defiance, undismayed by the power of darkness, undeterred when the heavens are brass, and undisturbed by the forecast of doom. His resources are without limits. His power is indomitable. His love is everlasting, and His purpose will prevail. He said, "I WILL BUILD MY CHURCH..." Trust Him. In His Omniscience, He knows everything. In His Omnipresence, He has been everywhere, and in His Omnipotence, He can do anything.

> *In His Omniscience, He knows everything. He has been everywhere. He can do anything.*

God has not stopped building and blessing his church. Therefore, it is our responsibility and privilege to:

1. Admit God's word is true.

2. Assume God will do what He said He would do.

3. Acknowledge the need for a miracle revival.

4. Arm yourself against doubt and doubters.

If you will follow God's instructions, he will move all obstructions. When you do all you can, God will do what you can't.

Action (30-60 Days Before Start Date)

1. Confirm the evangelist and date.

2. Prepare your budget.

3. Select a team of believers who know how to pray and pray. Send them an email requesting them to be a prayer partner with you and a prayer team to ask God for a mighty move of the Holy Spirit. A sample letter is enclosed along with a suggested prayer guide.

4. Meditate on the following comments by other men of God explaining the relationship between revival and prayer.

> *"The Bible and the record of history reveal that there has never been such a thing as a prayer-less revival." Dr. Louis L. King*

The Church is dying on its feet because it is not living on its knees." Leornard Ravenhill.

"When God is about to do a mighty new thing He always sets His people praying." Jonathan Edwards

"You can do more than pray after you have prayed; but you can never do more than pray until you have prayed." A.J. Gordon

"God does nothing except in response to believing prayer." John Wesley.

"Men may spurn our appeals, reject our message, oppose our arguments,   despise our persons, but they are helpless against our prayers." Sidlow Baxter

James 5:16 promises that the effectual fervent prayer of a righteous man avails much.

> **Nothing short of Divine intellect orchestrated prophetic details from beginning to end.**

5. Make copies of daily prayer guide and daily declarations, and distribute to your people with the encouragement that you pray for the coming revival every day.

6. Take hold of the promises of God and claim the move of God that He has promised. Get them embedded in your mind and spirit. Speak them in your prayers. Share them with other believers. Say them to the devil when assailed by doubt about the hope for revival. For your convenience, I have listed some exciting promises that give us confidence that we can have a mighty revival.

Luke 1:37 - For with God nothing shall be impossible.

Romans 4:21 – And being fully persuaded, that what he had promised, he was able also to perform.

Hebrews 6:18 – It was impossible for God to lie.

Numbers 23:19 – God is not a man that he should lie; neither the son of man that he should repent: hath he said, and shall he not do it? Or spoken, and shall he not make it good?

Matthew 18:19 – And again I say unto you, that if two of you shall agree on earth as touching anything that they shall ask, it shall be done for them of my Father which is in heaven. For where two or three are gathered together in my name, there am I in the midst of them.

Matthew 16:18 – Upon this rock, I will build my church; and the gates of hell shall not prevail against it. And I will give unto thee the keys of the kingdom of heaven; and whatsoever thou shalt bind on earth shall be bound in heaven; and whatsoever thou shalt loose on earth shall be loosed in heaven.

Mark 11:24 – Therefore I say unto you, what things soever you desire, when you pray, believe that you receive them, and you shall have them.

Mark 9:23 – Jesus said unto him, if you can believe, all things are possible to him that believeth.

Deuteronomy 4:29 – But if from thence you shall seek the Lord thy God, thou shall find him, if you seek him with all your heart and with all thy soul.

Romans 16:20 – And the God of peace shall bruise Satan under your feet shortly.

James 4:7 – Submit yourselves there for to God. Resist the devil, and he will flee from you.

Isaiah 65:24 – And it shall come to pass, that before they call, I will answer; and while they are yet speaking, I will hear.

Romans 8:26 – Likewise the Spirit also helps our infirmities: for we know not what we should pray for as we ought: but the Spirit itself makes intercession for us with groaning's which cannot be uttered. And he that searches the hearts knows what is the mind of the Spirit, because he makes intercession for the saints according to the will of God.

We stand with you and by faith declare, "We hear the sound of abundance of rain." Victory is on the way.

ADDENDUM

V. Daily Declarations

VI. 31 Days of United Prayer

**CLOSING PRAYER WITH YOU

Dear Lord, we take you at your word. We are agreeing together that you will break the bondage of sin in our personal lives, our church, city, and nation and orchestrate a Heaven sent breakthrough in our church and city in the very near future. Clothe us with the Holy Spirit, and validate your word with signs following. We declare revival is coming in the precious, powerful name of Jesus. Amen.

*To know what is right and not do it
is the worst cowardice."
-Confucius-*

Get ready. Get set. STOP!
(Preparing a Church for Revival)

<u>Timeline</u>: 0 to 30 days before the start date.

<u>Perspective</u>: *Preparation* is the act of preparing — getting ready, planning, training, or studying with a goal in mind. Benjamin Franklin said, "By failing to prepare, you are preparing to fail."

Proposal: "Commit thy way unto the Lord; trust also in him; and he shall bring it to pass." (Psalms 37:5) You do all that you can do, and trust God to do what you can't.

Get ready. Get set. STOP! That's not the way it goes. It's supposed to be: Get ready. Get set. Go! Far too often we launch a revival before we are ready.

It would never happen in the Olympics or a National Spelling Bee. These contestants are the product of long, arduous, disciplined preparation. They are given their best chance of winning by being properly prepared.

Alexander Graham Bell explained the importance of preparation when he declared, "Before anything else, preparation is the key to success."

Abraham Lincoln was driven by the need to prepare and summed it up like this. "If I had eight hours to chop down a tree, I'd spend six sharpening my axe."

So, let's examine these words again. Get ready. Get set. Is it go or stop? If we are not prepared for revival, WE SHOULD STOP AND SHARPEN OUR AXE.

Most of us are very familiar with II Chronicles 7:14, but we may not have detected the stop sign in the first word of the paragraph. It is "IF" my people….." In other words, it's not a go unless you have followed the instructions. Then it is a go which follows with these words. I will hear from heaven, and will forgive their sin and will heal their land.

Think of the "IF's" in several Scriptures that are stop signs calling for specific preparations.

- I John 1:9 – If we confess our sins, he is faithful and just to forgive us our sins, and to cleanse us from all unrighteousness.

- Matthew 18:19 – If two of you shall agree on earth as touching anything that they shall ask, it shall be done for them of my Father which is in heaven.

- Matthew 6:14 – If you forgive men their trespasses, your heavenly Father will also forgive you.

- Revelation 3:20 – Behold, I stand at the door and knock; if any man hear my voice, and open the door, I will come in…"

- Isaiah 1:19 – If you be willing and obedient, you shall eat the good of the land.

Don't ignore the stop signs and try to rush on to revival without doing your part. Preparation + God = A Successful Revival Effort.

Bobby Knight, the renowned basketball coach, saw the importance of preparation in this light. "The will to succeed is important, but what's even more important is the will to prepare."

After 400 years of silence, the New Testament opens with the booming voice of John the Baptist commanding the people of planet earth to "Prepare for God's arrival. Make the road smooth and straight!" (The Message – Matthew 3:3) The birth of God's Son was not a sudden impulse. Millenniums of planning and preparation went into minute details which were completed according to the plan. No details were left undone In Luke 24:27 Jesus said, Beginning with Moses and with all the prophets, He (Jesus) explained to them the things concerning Himself in the Scriptures.

Nothing short of a Divine intellect orchestrated the prophetic details from beginning to end. Born of a virgin. Born in Bethlehem. Betrayed by a colleague and friend. Sold for 30 pieces of silver, not gold. Spit upon. Fell under the load of the cruel cross. Died between two thieves. Offered gall and vinegar to quench his thirst. Felt forsaken by God. Bones were not broken, but His heart was. His side was ripped open by a sword. Buried in a rich man's tomb, and rose triumphantly from the dead. If we have any understanding of God whatsoever, we know that he was a Master Planner and Architect of time from the first day to the last day. It is meticulous and errorless.

The Book of Daniel is about more than lions, smoldering furnaces, and an armless hand scribbling a note on the wall. It's about a plan. God's plan. God revealed that plan to Daniel by telling him that His Son would be entering Jerusalem in 173,880 days from that very day. (Daniel 9:23-27) Kings and queens and kingdoms changed without numbers during the unfolding days, years, and dispensations, but God's plan didn't. It all came to pass according to God's plan.

His plan also reveals the final battle ground between good and evil, heaven and hell, and God and the devil. This was planned in eternity past and extends to eternity future with a clear picture of the time, place, combatants, and the grand and glorious outcome.

He planned the type of wood that would be used to build the Ark, the number of days and times that Jericho must be circled before the walls would fall, and when they were to shout not before. He planned the curtains of the tabernacle to be made of goat hair and in colors of blue, purple, and scarlet. He planned when Mary would become pregnant and give birth to Jesus. The Bible says, "When the fullness of time was come God sent forth his son…." (Galatians 4:4) It all went according to the plan.

If God is so precise and detailed in planning ahead, why do we find it difficult to do so with regards to revivals as well? I would like to purpose **THE TOP SIX EXCUSES.**

1. I DIDN'T KNOW I WAS SUPPOSED TO.

2. I DON'T KNOW HOW.

3. DOESN'T SEEM VERY SPIRITUAL AND A WASTE OF TIME.

4. EVANGELISTS HAVE REVIVAL IN A SUITCASE. It's their job. The fact is that the pastor prepares the church. The evangelists brings a message of God to the people, and God produces the increase.

5. PROCRASTINATION. I'll do it, but not now.

6. AMBIVALENCE. Uncertain as to value, and not sure people will attend.

We are not playing follow the leader. We are the leader, and as the leader "The commander must decide how he will fight the battle before it begins. He must then decide who he will use in the military effort at his disposal to force the battle to swing the way he wishes it to go; he must make the enemy dance to his tune from the beginning and not vice versa." Said Viscount Montgomery of Alamein.

Larry Bossidy made this astute observation. "Execution is the ability to mesh strategy with reality, align people with goals, and achieve the promised results." That was the main reason Jesus commanded his followers to depart from Golgotha, go to Jerusalem, and "wait for the promise of the Father." This was preparation time for the coming revival. It took ten days to get them ready for the Day of Pentecost to celebrate the birthday of the church. (Acts 2:7-12)

We know that only 120 people of the multitude that saw our Lord crucified obeyed the strategic plan. (Acts 1:15) I don't know everyone who was in that upper room when revival finally came, but the ones I do know surprises me. It was his own disciples and mother who needed to be there to get ready for the out pouring from the skies. Look at the guest list carefully, and you will probably be surprised also.

- There was Mary the mother of Jesus – the one who carried Him in her womb, wiped His dirty nose, and changed His diapers (Acts 1:14). She lived and ate with Him daily washed His clothes, cooked His meals and combed His hair. She was closer to him than about anyone else could have been, but she had somethings to deal with before she could be ready for what God was going to do. She had to deal with a bruised and broken heart and revulsion of a heartless crowd that found it amusing when her Son was mauled, mocked, and murdered. Getting over hurts and disappointments was and is an important part of getting ready for revival.

> *Getting over hurts and disappointments was a part of getting ready for revival.*

- Peter was there. (Acts 1:14-3) He was the Big Fisherman with a big, fat ego, and anger issues. A fisherman of the first century was a man's man, but a man's man had to be transformed into God's man. Fishermen were full of vigor and had boisterous tempers. Peter might have been a good, successful fisherman, but he was a poor example of Christian behavior. He didn't practice what he preached.

Christians are to be the Light of the world, but Peter must have turned the switch off when he attended a tail gate party and wanted to impress one of the young ladies at the camp fire. He left his religion at the altar and altered his conduct outside the four walls of the church. He talked a good talk in Sunday School but didn't walk the walk when and where it mattered the most. It's sad to say that similar situations have hindered the work of God in so many places. Peter needed to spend time alone with God before he took the platform to preach on the Day of Pentecost. Revivals and hypocrisy do not mix. Character does matter to God. A thriving fishing business did not qualify him to be an elder in the church of God.

Paul left no margin for error when he addressed eldership and deacons. "he must have a good report of them which are without…" (I Timothy 3:7)

> *Bad reputations can be a sword stabbed into the heart of revival and evangelism.*

Bad reputations can be a sword stabbed into the heart of revival and evangelism. Peter's reputation as a fisherman may have been so well known that he could have been a fisherman's guide, but his reputation as a Christian man must have been so tainted that it was a greater hindrance than a help in trying to reach the lost. I am inclined to believe that Peter was a member of the waiting crowd in the upper room working on his own short comings and having a change of heart before he could expect to change the world. Peter was in the getting ready brigade.

- Thomas was hunkered down and sequestered with 119 others in their cubby hole – not a glamorous cathedral. He was hiding with the other disciples after the resurrection and was still hiding before revival broke out in Jerusalem. His dubious doubting had to be resolved before he could be a spark to kindle the fire of revival. Doubters must become believers before we can expect God to show up in town.

- Matthew, the tax collector, was in the "waiting room" as well. Tax collectors were not the most loved men in town. They were known as thieves with a license to steal and did not live by the golden rule of loving one another. I don't know if he had to overcome the law of the jungle in favor of the law of love, but I do know he was with the "getting ready crowd." He no doubt had some wrongs to make right.

At the <u>end of 10 days of preparation, there was a DIVINE VISITATION.</u>

> *The little, upper room hideout became a geyser of God's glory, a fountain head of God's grace, and a powerhouse of God's favors.*

The Bible describes it like this. "And Suddenly..." (Acts 2:2) Preparation time was over. Divine Visitation time had arrived. The little, upper room hideout became a geyser of God's glory, a fountain head of God's grace, and a powerhouse of God's favors.

If God could send revival to jaded Jerusalem, God can send a revival to your city. Don't give up on the hope of revival until you give up on God.

- God can deliver revival to anyone, anywhere at any time. (Isaiah 44:3a)

- The promise of revival is clear. (Joel 2:23-25)

- The positive impact of revival is unquestionable. (I Thessalonians 1:9-10)

- The hindrances to revival can be recognized and removed. (Mark 11:23)

- The terms of revival are conditional. (II Chronicles 7:14)

- The passion for revival must be intensified. (Revelation 2:4)

- Revival is God's answer for polarization in the church. (Galatians 3:28)

- Revival will restore awe in worship, cheerfulness in giving, joy in singing, fire in preaching, and motivation to lead the lost to Christ.

Best of all, 3,000 people kept angels busy in paradise recording their names in the book of life. They were 6,000 legs out running the hounds of hell to find redemption through the Blood of the Cross.

Suddenly, all the preparation was worthwhile. Suddenly, the long, overlooked prophecy of Joel became front page news. Suddenly, conviction and contrition settled over the city that hosted the crucifixion of the Lord of glory. The tide turned. A city hardened by religiosity, ignorant of God's mercy and deaf to the message of grace found themselves in the grip of grace. Ordinary liturgy and normal church activity could not produce such an astonishing result. It took an over the top, supernatural visitation of God to penetrate the wall of resistance, overcome prejudice, convert the corrupt, and melt icy hearts.

> *There were 6,000 legs out running the hounds of hell to find redemption through the Blood of the Cross.*

This is the city that Jesus wept over and died in, It may appear to be one of those unreachable, unalterable, untouchable metropolitan populations that sing and dance on the crumbling edge of damnation. A city of heartless indifference and deadened moral sensibilities. Jesus knew what seemed to be the incorrigibility of this evil mecca and said, "You kill the prophets and stone them that are sent to you." (Matthew 23:37) But God shook this city like a bowl of Jell-O and snatched 3,000 souls from the clutches of the enemy in one 24-hour period. God can shake your city as well.

Get ready. Get set. STOP! Are you prepared for revival that will break the arm of the enemy, gladden the heart of God, increase the joy of angels, and set the captives of sin free? I join you in praying that your church and community will be impacted by a mighty visitation of God.

Action: 0 To 30 Days Before Start Date.

1. Send a copy of ABOUT THE EVANGELIST (XI) and request he/she fill it out and return it as soon as possible to: (church address)

   _____

   _____.

2. Send the evangelist a copy of ABOUT THE CHURCH (XII) for his/ her information.

3. Encourage the church to continue to pray earnestly for the coming revival. Be specific.

4. Finalize your revival budget (XII).

5. Select your altar workers, and train them in the manner that best suits you.

6. Finalize your advertising plans.

7. Post a simple, short note in your weekly bulletin announcing the coming date and naming the evangelist. Or begin to make a short, simple announcement from the pulpit.

8. Prayerfully consider preaching a message on being hungry for more of God.

This is a suggested outline for your sermon inspiration.

Are You Ready For Revival?
Take The Revival Readiness Test: Grade Yourself

Are you willing to do it God's way
even if it goes against your own way?
(John 14:15)

Are you willing to make hard choices?
(II Chronicles 7:14)

Are you willing to spend time alone with God
to reestablish intimacy with Him?
(Matthew 6:6)

Are you willing to pursue revival
at any cost to the glory of God?
(Esther 4:11-14)

Are you willing to subject you and your people
to the prophetic word that God has for you?
(Romans 11:22)

Are you so hungry for God that you can't hardly
live without more of Him?
(Matthew 5:6)

Are you willing to place God in the top priority
position of your life and ministry?
(Matthew 6:33)

Are you willing to give God all the glory
and not demand any for yourself?
(I Timothy 1:17)

It is either Stop or Go time, and you must make that choice. I urge you to keep in mind that failure always overtakes those who have the power to do without the will to act. Choice not chance will determine your destiny. Before you make your critical choice, I urge you to look to God who is the author and finisher of our faith to send us revival NOW; and rest your hopes and dreams in the hands of God. He is our:

- ✓ Sovereignty in every situation we face.
- ✓ Sufficiency for all our needs.
- ✓ Satisfaction of our deepest longings.
- ✓ Sympathy for our pain and suffering.
- ✓ Strength over all our enemies.
- ✓ Support for every crisis.
- ✓ Surety for every promise in the Bible.
- ✓ Subsistence for time and eternity.
- ✓ Supernatural lifestyle provider!

It's decision time just like it was for the Boston Celtics. With five seconds left on the clock and the score was tied with Seattle, time was called. As the team huddled on the side line to call one last shot, Larry Bird blurted out these words to these towering, sweaty, smelly giants of the basketball world, "Why don't you just give me the ball and tell everybody else to get....out of the way?" The coach was a bit miffed by his suggestion, and responded, "Larry you play, and I'll coach." Then he continues, "Dennis, you take it out and you get it to Kevin. Kevin, you get it to Larry and everybody else...get out of the way." Before the timeout was over, Bird leaves the huddle and went directly to Xavier who had been guarding him all night and told him a little secret. "Xavier, I'm getting the ball. I'm going to take two dribbles to the left. I'm going to step back behind the three-point line and stick it." And that is exactly what he did. So, when he stepped back behind the line and released the ball, as soon as he released it. His arm was still in the air going to the dressing room. Game over. Did I say, "Boston won the game?"

How do we have revival? Give the ball to GOD and get out of His way! He has told us what He can and will do, and all the cohorts of hell cannot stop Him.

You Give The Ball To God, And I Will Agree With You In Prayer.

"O Lord my God, your Word tells us that 'The effectual fervent prayer of a righteous man AVAILETH MUCH.' (James 5:16)

James didn't tell nor could he explain how much much is. It was much rain when Elijah prayed; much power when Paul and Silas prayed; much deliverance when Jonah prayed; much revelation when Stephen prayed, and God only knows how much will happen when we agree together in prayer.

Jesus said, "If two of you agree on earth as touching ANYTHING that they shall ask, it shall be done for them by my father which is in Heaven." Dear Lord, I am agreeing with my brothers and sisters in prayer for revival to break forth like the river flowing from the Throne of God that brings life to everything it touches. I am agreeing that the glorious light of the Gospel will shine into the darkest alleys in cities of sin. I am agreeing that corrupt politicians will have an encounter with God and bow down to the King of kings and Lord of Lords.

I am agreeing that all the attributes of God will form a canopy around and over believers and churches to save us from the onslaught of the enemies of the Cross. I am agreeing that people will forsake their sins and regain their forfeited inheritance which is to be heirs and joint heirs with Jesus Christ. I am agreeing that when Jesus returns, believers will be leaping for joy as they take wings and fly away to be forever with our Lord.

I am agreeing that the blind will see, the deaf shall hear, and the lame will not only walk but leap, dance, and praise God. I am agreeing that God will curse the devourer, unlock the treasure house of heaven, and pour out blessings that we cannot contain.

I believe and confess with my brothers and sisters that God's love is not limited, His redeeming grace is not rationed.

There are no borders to His blessings. There are no curbs to His compassion and no frailty in His faithfulness.

Now Father, do what your Son promised you would do – "It shall be done for them by my father which is in heaven." This I humbly but confidently ask in the precious, powerful name of Jesus. Amen."

ADDENDUM

(XI) About the evangelist/special speaker

(X)About the church

"Now unto him that is able to keep you from falling, and to present you faultless before the presence of his glory With exceeding joy. To the only wise God our Savior, be Glory and majesty, dominion and power, both now and ever. Amen." -Bible, Jude 24, 25

ADDENDUMS
I. You May Not Need a Revival If...

- Everyone in your church/city is saved.
- The demons of lust and pornography have been driven out of the city limits.
- The divorce court docket is blank at the court house.
- Rape and incest no longer exists.
- Thieves have been thwarted once and for all.
- Suicides have been reduced to zero.
- Drug addictions have disappeared.
- Your entire church congregation is prayed up and ready to go up.
- Corruption in government has been successfully resolved.
- All confessed believers are faithful tithers.
- You have more voluntary workers than you have jobs for them to do.
- Love and worship of Jesus is as passionate as God would have it be.
- Signs are following believers as the Scripture declares.
- The Fruit of the Spirit is alive and well.
- The Gifts of the Spirit are functioning regularly in your congregation.
- Prayer meetings draw as big a crowd as a picnic.
- Singing is neither traditional nor contemporary but simply Christ centered.
- Your church is hungry for intimacy with Jehovah.
- No one can find or think of anyone they need to forgive or receive forgiveness from.
- Holiness is in greater demand than making people happy.

Now you decide. Do you need a revival or not?

II. Work Sheet for Planning a Revival

Purpose For Revival:

Theme:

Preferable Date:

Preferable Days:
- ☐ Sunday through Sunday
- ☐ Sunday through Wednesday
- ☐ Wednesday through Sunday
- ☐ Sunday AM and PM
- ☐ Other – explain

Evangelists Under Consideration:

Name:	Number:	Email

Accommodations for the Evangelist:

Lodging Location:
Reservation Confirmation No:
Estimated Cost:
Meals Provided By:
Estimated Cost:
Travel Provided By:
Estimated Cost:
Honorarium:
Budget:

Revival Notes:

Worship Leader (Team):
Special Music:
Advertising Plan:

III. What is an evangelist?

The *evangelist* is one that travels from town to town and from church to church spreading the Gospel of Jesus Christ.

Sinclair B. Ferguson also defines another characteristic that all evangelists should have. He declared, "We best defend the Lord's glory by speaking first to Him about unbelieving men rather than speaking first ABOUT Him to unbelieving men." They know how to talk to God and have God listen.

The exact word "evangelist" is only listed two times in the New Testament but filled a dynamic purpose in the New Testament church. (Ephesians 4:11, II Timothy 4:5) As I did a search to discover a "model" or prototype, I found the one that our Lord called, "Phillip, the evangelist." Most of the details are recorded in Acts 8 which are bursting the seams with vital information that includes but is not limited to the following distinguishing trademarks.

1. They are a gift of God to the church. (Ephesians 4:11)
2. They are certified Kingdom workers. (II Timothy 4:5)
3. They are gifted to communicate with the educated as well as the illiterate; the high and mighty as well as the down and outer. (Acts 8:25-38)
4. They are driven to serve God faithfully in both urban, as well as, suburban communities. (Acts 8:25-38)
5. Signs and wonders often occur in their ministry. (Acts 8:6,7,13)
6. They are not money driven, but they should be showered by generous offerings where they minister. (Acts 8:14-22) These offerings/love gifts are their only source of support.
7. They preach Christ crucified—the sacrifice for sin. (Acts 8:5, 33, 35, 37)
8. They preach repentance and forgiveness of sin. (Acts 8:22)
9. They minister deliverance to set men free. (Acts 8:7)
10. Healings are not uncommon but should be expected. (Acts 8:7)
11. They take advantage of every opportunity to win people to Jesus both in and outside the church. (Acts 8:30-38
12. They are quick to baptize people in water and urge people to follow the Lord in water baptism. (Acts 8:38)

13. They go from place to place as the Spirit opens doors. (The entire chapter of Acts 8 is a travel log of Phillip, the evangelist's ministry.)

14. They are knowledgeable of the Scriptures. (Acts 8:29-33)

15. They are sensitive to the Holy Spirit. (Acts 8:39)

I am not attempting to make evangelist demi-gods, but I am recognizing them as an integral part of the Church of the Lord Jesus Christ. Many of them are gifted by the Holy Spirit to be especially used in Healing, Deliverance, Prophecy, Children, Faith, working of miracles only to mention a few.

Evangelists are the unique gift that God gave to the Church, and I want to tip my hat to the evangelists who are God's "almost forgotten" gifts. We thank God for the gift of eternal life, the gifts of the Spirit, the gift of faith, the gift of pastors, teachers, and sort of for apostles and prophets, but the congratulatory voices for evangelist are conspicuously silent. Many, not all, evangelist struggle for economic survival, acceptance, invitations to minister, and recognition for their place in the Church. Revivals have been quietly buried in unmarked graves. We rationalize, trivialize, and disfranchise evangelist from the five core gifts to the church.

I want to honor every evangelist, speak words of encouragement, and congratulate them for hearing and answering God's call and for fighting the good fight of faith. I want to do this because I know that saying nice things after they are called home will not inspire them to do cartwheels in their casket. No doubt, we have refrained for too long from saying "thank you," and I came to realize that unspoken gratitude is of no benefit to anyone on earth or in heaven. I bless each evangelist with financial favors, overflowing joy, unconditional love and acceptance, open doors that no man can shut, and an anointing from God that will empower them to confront the powers of darkness with the glowing light of the Gospel, to inspire saints to shout for joy, demand the devil to loose prisoners of sin, and set captives free. May the truth which falls from their lips light up communities with the glory of God and compel the infidels to stand up and take notice that God is in town.

IV. PASTOR/EVANGELIST RELATIONSHIP

The Bible basis: So then neither is he that plants anything, neither he that waters; but God that giveth the increase. Now he that plants and he that waters are one: and every man shall receive his own reward according to his own labor. For we are laborers together with God...God gave the increase. (I Corinthians 3:7-9, 6)

It is so easy to get so bogged down with who does what, when, where and why, and forget what's not pleasing to God. It reminds me so much of a scene at a rehearsal at the Metropolitan Opera House in New York City. A famous conductor, Arturo Toscanini, found it necessary to make a suggestion to the soloist which was not taken kindly. She quickly retorted, "I am the star of this performance!" Unperturbed, the seasoned but confident conductor said, "Madam, in this performance, there are no stars."

The same is true in revivals. There are no stars—except the Bright and Morning Star. We are not competitors. We are co-laborers. Pastor and evangelist are expected to exercise their gifts, but we must never forget that GOD GIVES THE INCREASE.

We are COMRADS. We are not sparing with each other, rivals, or competitors vying for positions. We are team mates, yokefellows, and prayer partners. I stand firmly on the words of Jesus who said, If two of you shall agree on earth as touching anything that they shall ask, it shall be done for them of my Father which is in heaven. (Matthew 18:19) Pastor and evangelist are two. Just two not ten or the entire church. Two. That relationship opens the door for a revival to be sent by the Father which is in heaven. Revival is an all-out war against the devil, and we can win when pastor and evangelist stand arm in arm in prayer. That strong relationship can break the stronghold of the devil, because it is then that God does what we can't do. It's called the power of two plus God!

The healthy relationship of a pastor and evangelist can be described by a snapshot in II Kings 10:15 in the Old Testament. I have read and re-read it over the years, and it becomes more relevant as time goes by. Examine it carefully.

"Is thine heart right, as my heart is with your heart." And Jehonadab answered, "It is." "If it be, give me your hand." And he gave him his hand. Hand in hand, side by side, they went to war together.

Mattie Stepanek summed up the supreme value of unity when she declared, "Unity is strength. When there are teamwork and collaboration, wonderful things can be achieved."

Pastors and evangelists should adhere to what Ignatius of Antioch said about unity. "Take heed, then, often to come together to give thanks to God, and show forth His praise. For when you assemble frequently in the same place, the powers of Satan are destroyed, and the destruction at which he aims is prevented by the unity of your faith."

Jesus simply used the words, "If two of you agree as touching anything…it shall be done for them by the Father which is in heaven." You want God to send a mighty revival? Agree together. This is a conscious choice and total commitment. What would this dynamic relationship look like in real life? How can it be attained?"

1. It begins with TOTAL HONESTY.

2. Be REAL.

3. Let your CARE show.

4. Be an ACTIVE LISTENER.

5. Embrace DIFFERENCES.

6. Acknowledge MUTUAL RESPECT.

7. Guard CONFIDENTIALITY.

8. PERSONALIZE the relationship. Know as much as you can about the other person, their family, hobbies, etc.

9. Make public comments of APPRECIATION for the other. This is especially true for an evangelist to honor the pastor in a sincere manner.

10. Avoid CRITICISMS AND CYNICISM.

11. PRAY with and for each other.

12. Send THANK YOU notes after the revival is over.

Remember the words of Mark Twain. "Kindness is the language which the deaf can hear and the blind can see." Relationships grow best in the soil of kindness.

V. DAILY DECLARATIONS

I declare that Jesus Christ is the one and only Son of the Most High God, and He is my Savior and Lord.

I declare that the Holy Spirit empowers me for effective ministry.

I declare that I serve a God that is unchangeable, unshakeable, and unstoppable.

I declare the Sovereignty of God will prevail in all matters pertaining to carrying out His purpose here on earth.

I declare God is working progressively, silently, successfully, and powerfully for me right now.

I declare that God has heard my prayers, and that answers are on their way.

I declare that I am blessed by our heavenly Father not lucky.

I declare that where God guides, He will provide.

I declare faith gives me the courage to face today with confidence and the future with high hopes.

I declare that God is faithful, and fear is futile.

I declare the Bible is my compass. If I follow it, I cannot go wrong.

I declare God's promises are true and will not fail.

I declare the absolute authority of God that cannot be successfully challenged or changed.

I make this declaration today in the precious, powerful name of Jesus.

VI. 31 DAYS OF DECLARATIONS AND UNITED PRAYER

1. Distribute Daily Declarations; explain process; individually recite declarations orally.

2. Recite declarations; pray for revival.

3. Recite declarations and pray for the pastor and board.

4. Recite declarations and pray for the peace and prosperity of every family.

5. Recite declarations and pray for dynamic worship.

6. Recite the declarations and pray the salvation of the lost.

7. Recite the declarations and pray for our country.

8. Recite the declarations and pray for financial miracles for those in need.

9. Recite the declarations and pray for our military and their families.

10. Recite declarations and pray for an out pouring of the Holy Spirit.

11. Recite the declarations and pray for missionaries through the world.

12. Recite declarations and pray for a forgiving spirit to fall upon us.

13. Recite the declarations and pray for signs and wonders to follow believers.

14. Recite the declarations and pray for God's will to be done on earth as in heaven.

15. Recite the declarations and pray for the healing power of God to be revealed today.

16. Recite the declarations and pray for the deliverance of addicts.

17. Recite declarations and pray the fruit of the Spirit to be evident among us .

18. Recite declarations and pray for the gifts of the Spirit to be operative in our church.

19. Recite the declarations and pray God's purpose for our lives will not be cancelled.

20. Recite the declarations and pray for forgiveness for our sins.

21. Recite declarations and pray that God will spare us of His judgment.

22. Recite declarations and pray that nothing will separate us from the love of God.

23. Recite the declarations and pray for a realization that Jesus is coming again.

24. Recite declarations and pray that God will rebuke the devourer for your sake.

25. Recite declarations and pray that God will hasten the answers to our prayers.

26. Recite declarations and pray no enemy formed against us will prosper.

27. Recite declarations and pray the gates of hell will not prevail against us.

28. Recite the declarations and pray that God will give us the oil of joy for our mourning.

29. Recite declarations and pray the blessings of the Lord to abound toward us in every way.

30. Recite declarations and pray God will heal the broken hearted and set the captives free.

31. Recite declarations and pray that God will bruise Satan under our feet shortly.

VII. Budget Information

It has been stated, "Failing to plan is the same as planning to fail." That principle holds true in the financial planning of a revival meeting. One service or multiple services, proper monetary preparation in advance will prove beneficial to all concerned. Such will enable any church, regardless of size or resources, to have a successful campaign with their evangelist/prophet of choice.

Example Revival Budget (Church of 50 attendees)

Three months in advance of the service(s), request that each member contributes $20 per month toward the budget. It should be noted that the amount requested is less than $1.00 per day!

This will produce $1,000 per month for the period of 3 months...$1,000 x 3 = $3,000.

As a pastor, one should receive an offering in EVERY service during the revival for the evangelist. This will allow visitors an opportunity to contribute, as well as church attendees who may desire to give a greater amount than the 90 day budget request.

While it will be at the discretion of the pastor how to disburse the budgeted monies (hotel, meals, travel expenses). ALL offering received during the revival should go to the evangelist in its entirety. The pastor should remember that the evangelist has no church to provide: retirement, vacation pay, health insurance, social security, special event honorariums (birthdays, anniversaries, pastor appreciation day, etc), or reimbursements to attend special ministry functions (conventions, councils, seminars, retreats). One should also remember, the evangelist's offering cannot be viewed as 100% salary. Rather, a portion of the offering most certainly goes toward the continued business expenses associated with operating the ministry.

Finally, the evangelist will not be able to minister every week of the year. Holidays and other unforeseeable circumstances will limit the number of engagements one can conduct. Having all of these things in mind, the pastor and church can prove a place of financial blessing and security through proper planning and support.

NOTE: This is a sample budget and can be adjusted accordingly to church size, the length of time needed to prepare, and the amount to be requested.

VIII. Ushers

The ministry of ushers is vital to the success of revival or any special services, and we would like to thank them in advance. Since they are probably the first face that people see when they enter the building, make it a good one. They should:

1. Be in place 30 minutes before service.
2. Be appropriately dressed.
3. Place a bottle of water on the pulpit for the guest speaker.
4. If the guest speaker enters the front door, take them to the pastor's office and lend your assistance to whatever they may request.
5. Welcome any person entering the building.
6. Greet and give special assistance to guests and make it a point to introduce them to others who may be in the entrance area.
7. Assist parents with a baby in the nursery or other departments if appropriate.
8. Seat the people in the auditorium.
9. Assist the pastor in distributing any necessary items.
10. Assist the pastor in receiving the offering.
11. Fill out the form: For the Record.
12. Be at the exit doors to say "Good night" to those departing.

Ushers should always remember and practice what Richelle E. Goodrich said. *"Service is a smile. It is an acknowledging wave, a reaching handshake, a friendly wink, and a warm hug. It's these simple acts that matter most, because the greatest service to a human soul has always been the kindness of recognition."*

IX. Musicians and Worship Team

Your role in the success of the revival is an invaluable component which must blend with the theme of the service and the message to be preached if that is known in advance. You are not just preparing people for the preaching. You are helping to usher them into the presence of God. Imagine that you are taking the audience by the hand and taking them to a rendezvous with the King of kings. Thank you for your ministry.

1. Arrive 30 minutes before the service.

2. Dress appropriately.

3. Do any tuning or warm up 30 minutes before the service begins.

4. The musicians and worship team should pray together at least fifteen minutes before the service.

5. Music should begin 10 minutes prior to beginning service.

6. Lead the congregation in worship. Get them involved. This is NOT A PERFORMANCE. Psalms 95:1 explains it like this. "O come, let us sing unto the Lord: let us make a joyful noise to the rock of our salvation."

7. Be pleasant.

8. Be joyful.

9. Be alert if called upon to participate otherwise.

"Expose your heart. Only then can you connect with your audience at the deepest level." -Kern Ho-

X. FOR THE RECORD

Date:	
Weather:	
Speaker:	
Subject:	
Attendance:	(nursery included)
Salvations:	
Rededications:	
Baptism in the Holy Spirit:	
Water baptism:	
Other:	

Date:	
Weather:	
Speaker:	
Subject:	
Attendance:	(nursery included)
Salvations:	
Rededications:	
Baptism in the Holy Spirit:	
Water baptism:	
Other:	

Date:	
Weather:	
Speaker:	
Subject:	
Attendance:	(nursery included)
Salvations:	
Rededications:	
Baptism in the Holy Spirit:	
Water baptism:	
Other:	

Date:	
Weather:	
Speaker:	
Subject:	
Attendance:	(nursery included)
Salvations:	
Rededications:	
Baptism in the Holy Spirit:	
Water baptism:	
Other:	

Date:	
Weather:	
Speaker:	
Subject:	
Attendance:	(nursery included)
Salvations:	
Rededications:	
Baptism in the Holy Spirit:	
Water baptism:	
Other:	

Date:	
Weather:	
Speaker:	
Subject:	
Attendance:	(nursery included)
Salvations:	
Rededications:	
Baptism in the Holy Spirit:	
Water baptism:	
Other:	

XI. About the Evangelist/Guest Speaker

(To be sent to evangelist to be completed and returned to pastor.)

Name:	
Address:	
City:	State & Zip:
Cell phone:	
Email:	
Web site (if any):	

The revival is scheduled to begin __/__/____. (date). When do you plan to arrive?

Will you be driving or flying?

If you fly, please provide us with the following information:

Airport:	
Airline:	Flight No:
Departure ETA:	Arrival ETA:

Will your spouse/family be traveling with you? ☐ Yes ☐ No.

What is your spouse's name?

Please give us the names and age of your children.

Please send us the following items as soon as possible so that we can include it in our advertising package.
- ☐ Bio
- ☐ Copy ready photo
- ☐ 2-3 minute video clip with an enthusiastic greeting, etc.
- ☐ Any other pertinent information that you wish to send.

What are your favorite fruits, snacks, etc.?

What are your favorite foods?

Do you prefer a hand microphone if available?
☐ Yes ☐ No ☐ No Preference

Do you need a book table? ☐ Yes ☐ No.
If yes, is one 8-foot table sufficient? ☐ Yes ☐ No.

Do you have your own music for each service? ☐ Yes ☐ No

Will you be bringing any muscial or other equipment with you for the service(s)? ☐ Yes ☐ No.

If yes, how much space do you need on the platform?

Do you want our music department to assist you in the altar service? ☐ Yes ☐ No
If so, please advise us accordingly.

Will you have need of a screen, etc.? If yes, please explain what you will need.

When will you be leaving for your next appointment?

XII. ABOUT OUR CHURCH:

(To be completed by pastor and sent to evangelist/special speaker.)

Name of Church:	
Address:	
City:	State & Zip:
Church web site (if any)	
Pastor Name:	
Pastor Cell:	
Pastor Email:	
Pastor's Spouse:	
Children names and age(s)	
Name of our city/community:	
Population:	Size of our Church:
Sunday AM Average Attendance:	

Normal Service Schedule:

Sunday AM:
Sunday PM:
Wednesday Night:
Other:

Dress for Pastors:
Number of Revivals Each Year:
Our Revival/Special service(s) with you is scheduled __/__/____

Provided Accommodations:

Food Arrangements:

Compensation Procedure:

Travel Expenses Policy:

Sound System and Technology Capabilities:

Book Table/Sales Policy:

Our basic format for a revival/special guest service:

Welcome:
Worship:
Prayer:
Special music:
Evangelist/Special Guest :
Altar Service:

Our services are recorded?:　☐ Yes　☐ No.

About The Author

Bob Brock has 60 years of experience in a variety of ministries and adds a deep wealth of practical knowledge to the subject of revival. Bob has served the church as a leading pastor, directed statewide youth organization, is a nationally known evangelist, seminar and convention speaker, personal coach to countless pastors, developer of church resources, author and friend to ministers of all ages. He and his wife reside just outside of Fort Worth, Texas and continue to pray for a God sent, Holy Ghost inspired, and life changing visitation of God.

God Got His Hands Dirty is his second published work. His first book, *The Triumph of the Cross* will soon be back in print. *Saying Goodbye; Funeral Sermon Treasure Chest* will be available Fall 2017.

If you would like email notifications about this author's upcoming published works, please signup for Empowered Publication's Author Newsletter at www.empowered.news .

CPSIA information can be obtained
at www.ICGtesting.com
Printed in the USA
FFOW01n1922270617

9 781943 033539